God, Government, and the Road to Tyranny

A Christian View of Government and Morality

by

Phil Fernandes
Eric S. Purcell
Kurt Rinear
Rorri Wiesinger

PRESS

In Memory of

Marvin Maguires (1945-2002).

A man who loved his God,

his family,

and his freedom.

TABLE OF CONTENTS

PREFACE

====================

It has been over 20 years since Francis Schaeffer wrote *A Christian Manifesto*. Now a new generation of Christians needs direction concerning the Christian view of government and morality. *God, Government, and the Road to Tyranny* can provide that direction as the pages of the 21st century unfold.

America and Western culture have mistakenly proclaimed "the death of God," and the consequences of this foolish pronouncement have begun to appear. Human governments grow larger, individual freedoms are lost, and the push towards a one world government continues.

The authors of this book declare what God intended human government to be and show how man, in his lust for power, has failed to promote good government. The authors warn of the coming death of western civilization as contemporary man, by rejecting God, has embarked on the godless and bloody "road to tyranny."

CHAPTER 1

THE BIBLICAL BASIS FOR HUMAN GOVERNMENT

by Phil Fernandes

THE BEST POSSIBLE GOVERNMENT

According to the Bible, the best possible government is a one-world government ruled by a perfect and all-powerful King. We will receive that government when the Lord Jesus (the perfect, all-powerful King) returns and brings the Kingdom of God to earth (Revelation 11:15; 19:11-16). The Bible teaches that He will reign over the entire earth for 1,000 years (Revelation 20). After that, He will reign over the entire universe for all eternity (Revelation 21 and 22).

Until Jesus returns, a one-world government headed by a less-than-perfect king or committee would be the worst possible form of government. Billions of people would be at the mercy of the sinful, greedy desires of the one ruler or one group of rulers. If the world ruler is demon-possessed, this only magnifies the wickedness. The Bible teaches that in the last days a demon-possessed man—the Antichrist— will rule the entire earth. He will persecute the church and put to death those who do not accept his mark on their forehead or right hand (Revelation 13). He will demand that he be worshiped as God (2 Thessalonians 2). Billions will be slaughtered under this ultimate reign of terror.

The question remains: Until Jesus returns and establishes God's Kingdom on the earth, what is the best form of human government? This book tries to answer that question—it attempts to discuss the Christian view of government and morality. This work is not exhaustive, and further thought in this area is encouraged. Unfortunately, Christians are often quick to engage in political activism without first building a Christian philosophy of government. The consequence of this knee-jerk mentality is that Christians often back a political party or platform without thinking through the complex issues that are involved. Without a carefully thought-out Christian philosophy of government, they have no grid through which they can intelligently interpret the issues.

It is our hope that this book will help. Although much of this book was originally a collection of essays (dealing with government, morality, and religion) that were written over a period of several years, the material has been updated and edited to form a unified theme—a Christian view of government and morality.

HUMAN GOVERNMENT WAS INSTITUTED BY GOD

The first thing we need to note is that human government was not man's idea. Human government was instituted by God. The pre-flood wickedness of Noah's day caused God to flood the earth and destroy a large portion of the human race. Noah and his family were the only humans to survive the flood. After the flood, to prevent human wickedness from rising to its pre-flood level, God instituted human government. Immediately following the flood, God allowed man to kill and eat animals, but warned man that "Whoever sheds man's blood, by man his blood shall be shed, for in the image of God, He made man" (Genesis 9:6). God alone has the right to judge the wicked since He alone is just. Still, to enhance the survival of the human race, God delegated to man a portion of His authority to judge the wicked by instituting human government.

CREATION: HUMAN LIFE IS WORTH PROTECTING

Second, the Bible teaches that God created men and women in His image (Genesis 1:26-27). This means that human life is sacred. The sanctity of human life means that human life is valuable—it is worth protecting.

Most evolutionists are not anarchists—they acknowledge the need for human government; but if humans were not created in God's image, then human life is not sacred. Human life would not be worth protecting. If evolution is true, then survival of the fittest would be the reigning ideology. Human government would be without justification. In a universe without God, there are no human rights.

Human government implies that human life is sacred and is therefore worth protecting. This makes no sense without the biblical doctrine of Creation. Since our society has rejected the doctrine of Creation, the sanctity of human life has been ignored. Hence, abortion, infanticide, and euthanasia are being practiced in America today.

THE FALL: HUMAN LIFE NEEDS PROTECTING

Even though man was created in God's image, there would still be no need for human government if mankind had not fallen into sin. Therefore, the third issue we need to discuss is the Fall of mankind (Genesis 3). The Bible teaches that, though man and woman (Adam and Eve) were created perfect by God, they fell into sin by disobeying God in the Garden of Eden. Because they sinned, their nature became corrupted. Adam and Eve passed this corrupted, fallen, sinful nature to their descendants (Romans 5:12). We are all conceived in sin (Psalm 51:5) and are therefore sinners.

Because we are sinners, we often infringe upon the God-given rights of other human beings. Therefore, the biblical doctrine of the Fall shows us that not only is human life worth protecting, but it needs protecting. Without both biblical doctrines of Creation and the Fall, there is no basis for human government or human rights.

Many liberal politicians want increasingly larger government, yet they do not believe man is fallen and sinful. The fact of the matter is this: if man is not fallen, then there is no need for human government, let alone big human government. Liberal politicians should be anarchists (those who oppose any and all government) rather than proponents of large government.

HUMAN GOVERNMENT MUST BE LIMITED IN ITS POWER

The fourth and final point we need to stress is that human government must be limited in its power. In other words, the Bible opposes big human government. Human government has a limited role—it is not the solution to every problem we face. Human government tries to replace God when it attempts to solve every human problem. It is idolatry (worship of a false god) to look to government to solve all our problems (i.e., poverty, health care, education, etc.). Only God can solve all our problems; only He knows what is best for us; only He deserves our worship and total dependence (Psalm 118:8-9).

The reason why human government power needs to be limited is that the leaders of human governments are sinful, fallen humans. Therefore, we need to be protected from government officials themselves.

Our founding fathers understood this biblical principle. For this reason, they set up our constitutional system of checks and balances and the separation of powers to limit the power of government officials. The powers of the federal government were divided between three branches of government: the executive, the legislative, and the judicial. These three branches of the federal government were given ways to check (limit) the power of the other branches so that all the power would not fall into the hands of one individual or one group of individuals. The power would be balanced between the three branches. Powers were also divided between the federal government and the state governments (the tenth amendment to the US constitution). The final limit or check of the power of the federal government is the right to bear arms (the second amendment). If our government becomes tyrannical and infringes upon our God-given rights, then the people of the United States would have the right to revolt and overthrow the US government. Of course, our founding fathers believed that revolution should only be considered as a last resort.

The Bible also limits the power of human government by limiting the role of human government. The Bible does not teach that it is the job of government to feed the hungry, heal the sick, and reform criminals. (In fact, these are acts of mercy—roles that God has given to the church. Presently, the governments of this world are attempting, whether consciously or unconsciously, to replace the church. Big government is becoming a religion.) God instituted human government for the purpose of protecting human life and human rights by punishing those who infringe upon the rights of others (Genesis 9:6; Romans 13:1-7). Therefore, human government is God-ordained, and we are to submit to human government (Mark 12:17; Romans 13:1-7; 1 Peter

2:9-17) except when it demands from us only what rightly belongs to God (Exodus 1; Joshua 2; Acts 5:29). When human government outlaws the preaching of the Gospel, orders the killing of innocent humans, or demands our worship, we must remain faithful to Jesus and resist the governing authorities. At a time when the Roman Empire forced people to say, "Caesar is Lord," Christians refused to obey the governing authorities and instead replied "Jesus is Lord" (Romans 10:9). When human government goes beyond its biblical role and tries to play God, the Christian must resist and remain faithful to God. God alone is the ultimate authority, not human government.

The rest of this book will look at how Christians should view different aspects of government and morality. Christians should allow their biblical world view to determine their views concerning government, society, and morality. God has called us to be a separate and holy people (2 Corinthians 6:14-18; 1 Peter 1:14-16; 2:9-17). Therefore, we must oppose the wickedness of the evil world system and seek God's righteousness (1 John 2:15-17; Matthew 6:33).

CHAPTER 2

THE CHRISTIAN ROOTS OF THE U.S. GOVERNMENT

by Phil Fernandes

S ome people deny that America was built upon a Christian foundation. However, if one looks closely at the founding documents of this great country one will clearly see that the Christian world view deeply influenced the establishment of America as a free and independent nation.

THE DECLARATION OF INDEPENDENCE

The vibrant Christian faith of the first settlers to this country (i.e., the Pilgrims) and the fact that the first schools founded in America were all Christian reveal the predominance of the Christian world view in the lives of the early colonists. But when one examines the Declaration of Independence, the U.S. Constitution, and the Bill of Rights, the power of the biblical world view in early American life becomes even more evident.

In the Declaration of Independence, the founders spoke of "the laws of nature and of nature's God." According to constitutional lawyer Herb Titus, the founding fathers borrowed this phrase from Blackstone's *Commentaries on the Laws of England*. Titus points out that the phrase was a well-known 18th century common law phrase that meant the moral laws of God revealed both in the consciences of men and in the Bible.[1] Hence, in the founding of this nation, our forefathers appealed to the biblical view of morality (as it applied to both individuals and governments).

The founding fathers based their political ideology upon the belief that "all men are created equal." This meant that they acknowledged that the Creator God exists and that human government should be based upon belief in Him as Creator. It also affirmed the biblical teachings that all humans were created in God's image, that they were given unalienable rights, are equal in God's eyes, and, therefore, should be treated as equals by the governing authorities.

By acknowledging human rights as unalienable, the founders understood these rights to be God-given. Therefore, they could not be taken away by other men or governments. God instituted human governments to protect these God-given, unalienable rights, not to infringe upon them. The colonists believed they had the right to break from England because the British government refused to respect the unalienable rights of the colonists.

The Declaration of Independence spells out these unalienable rights as the rights to life, liberty, and the pursuit of happiness. The right to life meant that since human beings were created in God's image, human life was sacred. Innocent human life is to be protected by human governments—the government is not to take innocent human life. The right to liberty meant that God gave man free will and that human governments should protect a man's freedom to believe as he wishes and do as he desires so long as he does not infringe upon the rights of others. The right to the pursuit of happiness did not mean that the government is to guarantee a person's happiness, but that the government was to respect a person's freedom to be all that he believes God wants him to be. This includes, but is not limited to, the right to enjoy the fruit of one's labor, the right to choose one's profession, and the right to own property.

In short, the Declaration of Independence assumes a biblical view of God, government, man, and morality. God has given man rights and has instituted human government to protect these sacred rights. When a government fails to protect these rights and instead infringes upon the rights of its citizens, as a last resort, God may choose to replace the tyrannical government with a more biblically-based government. This, believed the founding fathers, was what the American revolution was all about.

THE U.S. CONSTITUTION

The U.S. Constitution[2] is an extremely brief document, and there is a good reason for this. The founding fathers took seriously the biblical doctrine of the Fall of mankind—they were very aware of the sinfulness of humans, especially government officials. They agreed with Lord Acton's statement, "Power corrupts, and absolute power corrupts absolutely." Because of this, the founding fathers sought to limit the powers of the federal government so that the people would not be at the mercy of the sinful nature of one leader or one group of leaders. Hence, the U.S. Constitution is a very short document because the federal government was given few powers; most of the power remained with the people and the state governments.

The Constitution further limited the power of the federal government by establishing a separation of powers. The power was not only divided between the people, the states, and the federal government, but the little power given to the federal government was split between the three branches of that government (executive, legislative, and judicial). A system of checks and balances was created in order to encourage one branch of the federal government to limit the power of the other two branches, while having its own power limited by the other two branches.

THE BILL OF RIGHTS

The first ten amendments to the U.S. Constitution were produced not to increase the size and power of the federal government, but to clearly annunciate rights and freedoms of individuals that the federal government could not take away or infringe upon.[3] It cannot be over stressed: the Bill of Rights speak of the rights of the individual; it does not address the powers of the federal government; in fact it clearly states what the federal government *cannot* do.

The founding fathers realized that God instituted human government to serve man, not to enslave man. Human government was to dedicate itself to the limited role of protecting its citizens' rights; it was not to attempt to take those rights away.

As the decades passed, America began to lose sight of its Christian roots. Further amendments to the constitution had the exact opposite effect on human rights than the Bill of Rights had. The Bill of Rights focused on the rights of the individual. The freedom of the individual to speak his views, worship according to the dictates of his conscience, publicly assemble, and petition the government were proclaimed. A person's right to bear arms and to protect himself from evil individuals or a tyrannical government was recognized. The Bill of Rights did not claim that the federal government was giving these (as well as other) rights to individuals; instead, the Bill of Rights acknowledged these rights as unalienable, God-given rights, and that the federal government had no right to infringe upon them.

Later amendments to the Constitution began to give the federal government more and more power—power that was not granted to the federal government in the Constitution. The tenth amendment clearly states that any power not given to the federal government in the U.S. Constitution automatically is reserved for the people and the state governments. In essence, any amendment to the constitution, or any ruling in federal courts, that gives additional powers to the federal government is unconstitutional. An example of this is the federal government's increasing control over public education. Since the U.S. Constitution does not delegate any power to the federal government concerning education, control over public education resides with the people and the state governments. Hence, the U.S. Department of Education is itself unconstitutional.

CONCLUSION

The Declaration of Independence, the U.S. Constitution, and the Bill of Rights reveal that America was founded upon Christian principles. The founders affirmed belief in God as Creator and man as created in His image. They acknowledged the sinfulness of man and the need to limit the power of human government. They understood that God instituted human government to protect the rights of man, not to enslave man. In more recent times, as the Christian world view no longer dominates the thought of our leaders, the size and power of the federal government has increased and human freedom is being stifled. Let us pray that our nation returns to the God who has blessed us so abundantly; for, without repentance, America will continue to travel down the ungodly, de-humanizing road to tyranny.

ENDNOTES

[1] Herbert W. Titus, *The Declaration of Independence: The Christian Legacy* (Chesapeake: Titus Publications, 1995), 6-9.

[2] John Eidsmoe, *Institute on the Constitution: Study Syllabus* (Bridgewater, Virginia: American Foundations Publications, 1995). Lawrence Patton McDonald, *We Hold These Truths* (Marietta, Georgia: The Larry McDonald Memorial Foundation, 1975).

[3] Ibid.

CHAPTER 3

IS MAN AN ANIMAL?

by Phil Fernandes

Our founding fathers believed that "all men are created equal." They did not mean that all men share the same talents or have the same potential. They meant that all men and women were created in the image of God. Therefore, all men are equal in God's eyes and deserve equal rights and freedoms. Our founding fathers believed that God instituted human government to protect the God-given rights of each individual. Because these rights were given to men by God they were called "unalienable rights." Governments were to protect these rights; they did not have the authority to take these rights from men. Rights such as life, liberty, and the pursuit of happiness were God-given. What God has given, reasoned the founders of this great country, let no man take away.

The belief that God created man formed the basis for the political/economic experiment called the United States of America. No people in the history of human government have enjoyed greater freedom than the fortunate citizens of this land. Still, the foundation for this freedom has been slowly deteriorating for several generations. The doctrine of atheistic evolution has replaced the belief in God as Creator. The political and economic implications are clear. For if man was created by God, then the equal rights of all citizens should be protected. However, if there is no God and if we evolved from apes, then men are not equal. Some of us are probably "more evolved" than others. Maybe the "more evolved" ones (they would probably rather be called the "enlightened ones") should make the decisions for the less fortunate people. In short, creation by God implies human equality, while evolution encourages a "survival of the fittest" mentality.

If America is to return to its former status as the land of the free, its people will have to recover their lost belief in God as Creator. This belief must not be a mere verbal acknowledgement of God as Creator, but a conviction that effects the way we Americans think and act. Until that day comes, our freedoms will continue to dwindle.

Though we have been told that science has proven evolution to be true, this is not the case, for the second law of thermodynamics (energy deterioration) has shown that the universe is running out of usable energy; it is winding down. However, if the universe is winding down, it had to be wound up. It had to have a beginning at which time all its energy was usable. But, if the universe had a beginning, then something separate from the universe had to cause it to come into existence. For from nothing, nothing comes. Therefore, some eternal Being that is separate from the universe had to cause it to come into existence.

Evolution teaches spontaneous generation, the belief that life randomly evolved from non-life. But, this is impossible for the simplest unit of life, a single cell, contains enough genetic information to fill one volume of an encyclopedia. An encyclopedia cannot evolve into existence; it needs an intelligent mind to design it. Therefore, whatever Being caused the universe to come into existence must be an intelligent Being.

Modern science has not proven evolution. Instead, it has shown us that an intelligent Being caused the universe to come into existence. Hence, modern science favors the concept of creation by God, not the false belief of evolution. Once the majority of Americans recognize this fact (and live their lives in accordance with it), then and only then can we hope to have our freedom back. Until then, it will continue to be "the survival of the fittest."

CHAPTER 4

IS GOD ESSENTIAL TO FREEDOM?

by Phil Fernandes

O ur founding fathers acknowledged God as the Creator. They believed that His laws were above all human government. They recognized that the Lord had given men and women "unalienable" rights, and that He had instituted human government for the purpose of protecting those rights. Since the rights of the individual were given by God and not derived from the government, the government had no authority to eradicate these rights.

God's moral laws were seen as eternal and unchanging. They were absolute standards to which both citizens and leaders had to submit. The laws of this nation were not based upon the arbitrary and changing decisions of man; instead, they were established by the unchanging nature of the Almighty God. Even the government itself had to adhere to the commands of the Supreme Being.

Unfortunately, the intellectual climate has changed

drastically in this country. A secular view of government has replaced the traditional idea of a God-ordained government. This secular view recognizes no God above human government—there are no divine laws that exist above the government; hence, the government is not accountable to God. The government has become the ultimate now that God (the real ultimate Being) is ignored.

Under the former view of government, America prospered. The citizens of this country experienced a level of freedom unheard of throughout human history. The question must therefore be asked, "Without acknowledging God as above our government, can we remain free?" The answer appears to be "no." Once God is taken out of the equation, the government begins to play God. Government officials are answerable to no one since the government itself becomes the highest authority. No power is recognized above the government. Arbitrary laws are created which declare things to be right or wrong merely because the government has deemed them as such.

Two examples come to mind of governments that refused to acknowledge the existence of God and His laws as above all human governments. Nazism under Hitler and Communism under Stalin are extreme cases. Still, these two regimes are the natural consequence of the unchecked power of human authority. The horrible crimes committed against humanity in both cases were beyond description. Millions of innocent men, women, and children were tortured and murdered. Yet, the actions of Hitler and Stalin were "legal." For there was no authority recognized as above the government through which to judge the government. In Germany, Hitler was the law; in Russia, Stalin was the law. There were no recognized divine laws above the government to judge the human laws of those governments.

If a person responds by saying that things can never get that bad in America, then this person only shows his or her ignorance concerning the horrors of human history and the sinfulness of mankind. As Lord Acton once said, "Power corrupts, and absolute power corrupts absolutely." Our founding fathers echoed this proclamation as they limited the power of our leaders. We must learn the lessons that history teaches its future generations. We must accept the fact that *any attempt to establish a free society is doomed to failure if God's laws are not acknowledged as being above the government itself.*

America must return to the God who blessed her so abundantly. She must recognize that there is always a Stalin or a Hitler behind the curtain, waiting to be revealed. America is not immune to the disease of tyranny. It can infest any nation. If the United States government does not submit itself once again to God's unchanging laws, there will be no freedom. For without recognition of God as the supreme Lawgiver, there can be no freedom. God is essential to human freedom.

CHAPTER 5

THE CHRISTIAN VIEW OF COMMUNISM

by Phil Fernandes

OVERVIEW OF MARXIST COMMUNISM

Some Christians have argued that the early church was a communistic society and that the biblical form of government is some type of communism. However, this is clearly not the case. Communism is at its core a godless system that has led to the violent deaths of approximately 100 million innocent people during the twentieth century.[1]

In this essay, we will look at the thought of Karl Marx and Friedrich Engels and show that their ideas, as well as the Soviet and Gramscian versions of communism, are anti-Christian. Christians should oppose communism just as we should oppose all that is evil.

Marx and Engels viewed the history of human societies as the struggle for wealth and private property. Human history is determined by the relationships of labor (the working class) to ownership.[2] This is called economic determinism, the theory that economic factors control the movement of history and the destiny of man. Marx and Engels saw the future determined by the class struggle between the proletariat (the working class) and the bourgeoisie (the owners of the means of production). History was unfolding from one economic system to another. In the end, profit and private ownership—both are considered evil by Marxists— would be removed and a perfect, classless society would be ushered in. The arrival of the final utopian stage of human history could be accelerated through the revolution of the working class.[3] Christianity rejects economic determinism and teaches that human history is determined by man's relationship (or lack thereof) to God, and God's work of redemption through the Lord Jesus Christ.

Marx and Engels accepted a simplified version of Hegel's dialectic. The philosopher Hegel saw history as the unfolding and synthesizing of ideas. The simplistic (but mistaken) interpretation of Hegel's thought, accepted by Marx and Engels, viewed history in terms of a reigning idea (the thesis) that dominated an age. This thesis would be opposed by the antithesis, an alternative theory that contradicted the thesis. Rather than one idea being true and the other false, the two contradictory ideas would be synthesized to produce a new truth (the synthesis). Though Hegel's philosophy was idealistic (it denied the reality of the physical realm; only ideas exist), Marx and Engels combined the dialectic with their philosophy of materialism (only material things are real). This became known as dialectical materialism. Marx and Engels believed that God did not exist and that religion is harmful—it is a drug that intoxicates man and dulls his senses so that he does not see the economic alienation he is suffering. If man was to be truly free, than religious superstitions would have to be overcome.[4]

Marx and Engels accepted Darwin's theory of evolution

and the idea of the survival of the fittest. Because they viewed the ruling class as those who owned the means of production, Marx and Engels believed that the governments of the world needed to be overthrown by the working class. When the working class came to power they were to rule over their society (the dictatorship of the proletariat) until the day when the classless society could be achieved.

In Marxist Communism, private property (i.e., private ownership) had to be abolished.[5] The workers (i.e., the new state—the government) were to own all things in common. Another communist goal is the abolition of the family. The new state (the dictatorship of the proletariat) was to raise and educate (i.e., indoctrinate) the children.[6] Eventually, a one-world communist government would come into existence, and then the proletariat will relinquish their control and usher in the classless society.[7]

Marx and Engels believed that the end justified the means (pragmatism). However, Christianity teaches that it is wrong to do evil in an attempt to bring about good; the end does not justify the means. But even the goal of communism (the classless society) is evil from a biblical perspective, for the Bible teaches that, due to the Fall of mankind and in order to protect the God-given rights of man, God instituted human government. Evil needs to be restrained; humans need to be protected. In short, the real problem is the sinful heart of man, not profit or private ownership.

SOVIET COMMUNISM

Many people claim that Marxist communism would work if given a chance, but that Soviet communism is a perversion of Marxist communism. In reality, Soviet communism is much closer to Marxist communism than most people realize. The main difference is that the Soviets rejected the dictatorship of the proletariat. The Soviets replaced it with a dictatorship headed by the professional revolutionaries who had overthrown the government, believing that the working class was not equipped to lead a government.[8] But even if the Soviets allowed the working class to rule, any dictatorship will enslave people and destroy lives, for "power corrupts and absolute power corrupts absolutely." Also, it is hard to envision what a dictatorship of the working class would look like. Presumably, representatives of the working class would have to assume leadership positions in the "transitional" dictatorship. In essence, it would not be the working class ruling; rather it would be dictators who supposedly have the best interests of the working class in mind. It is hard to see how this would produce any better results than the mass slaughter of human beings produced by Soviet-style communism. And finally, it is highly unlikely that any dictators would relinquish power once all the governments of the world had been overthrown by communists. In short, Marxist communism, if put into practice, would fare no better than Soviet communism.

GRAMSCIAN COMMUNISM

Italian communist Antonio Gramsci wholeheartedly accepted the Marxist goal of the utopian society, but he believed that Marx and Engels were unrealistic in their belief that the working class would revolt against their rulers. Gramsci understood the large role that religion (i.e., Catholicism and Protestantism) played in the lives of Europeans. He believed that, due to their belief in the hereafter, the workers would not revolt.

Therefore, Gramsci believed that the Marxist goals should be attained through evolution (gradual change of a society) rather than revolution.[9] Gramsci understood that religion was too powerful to overthrow from the outside. Hence, Gramsci proposed that religion be infiltrated by communists and be taken over by them. Religion could not be defeated by communism, but it could be used by communism. In Central America, this infiltration and redefining of Christianity by communists has become known as Liberation Theology. In Liberation Theology, Jesus is not the Savior of our souls; instead, He is the deliverer of the poor and the oppressed. In short, the Jesus of Liberation Theology is the greatest Marxist revolutionary who ever lived. He offers no heaven in the hereafter, only a communist society in the here and now.

Gramsci also believe that the schools, the media, and the arts needed to be infiltrated and taken over by communists. Many of our current American leaders could be classified as Gramscian communists. They desire larger and larger government with more and more government control, but they do not want to achieve this all powerful state through revolution (Marxism); instead they want to achieve their goals through gradual changes within society (Gramscian communism).

45 GOALS OF THE AMERICAN COMMUNIST PARTY

In the 1950's, the Soviet Union detailed 45 goals to take over America from within. These goals have been entered into the congressional record and discussed at congressional hearings. W. Cleon Skousen served for 16 years in the FBI. In his book *The Naked Communist* he lists and discusses these 45 goals.[10] Some of these goals include: total disarmament of the United States military, the takeover of one or both of the U.S. political parties, gaining control of the schools and the media, encouraging sexual promiscuity and homosexuality as freedom of speech issues, discrediting the U.S. Constitution and the Founding Fathers, eliminating prayer and religious expression in the public schools, discrediting the family, promoting easy divorce, and enlarging the size of the U.S. government by centralizing control over different aspects of culture (education, welfare, health, etc.).

Even though the Soviet Union has supposedly collapsed, these goals still present a threat to our freedoms. Big government enslaves; it is irrelevant whether or not it goes by the official name of communism.

WAS THE EARLY CHURCH COMMUNISTIC?

The Bible tells us that the early church shared "everything in common" (Acts 2:41-45). Does this mean that the early church was a communist society? The answer is no, for the members of the early church voluntarily shared their private property with others. This is compassionate capitalism, not communism. In communism, private property is taken by force and distributed by the dictators. (In practice, the dictators always allot much more property and wealth to themselves then to their people.)

God wants Christians to cheerfully give to others, but He did not institute human government to redistribute wealth. He instituted human governments to protect man and his God-given rights, not to enslave man. God gave man dominion over the earth, and this entails the private ownership of property. God did not give human government dominion over the earth. God intended human government to serve its citizens, not to enslave them.

ENDNOTES

[1] This has been documented in *The Black Book of Communism* (Cambridge, Massachusetts: Harvard University Press, 1999).

[2] Ian P. McGreal. ed. *Great Thinkers of the Western World* (New York: Harper Collins, 1992), 379.

[3] David McLellan. ed. *Karl Marx: Selected Writings* (Oxford: Oxford University Press, 1977), 231, 246.

[4] Ibid., 64.

[5] Ibid., 232.

[6] Ibid., 234, 235.

[7] Ibid., 235.

[8] Thomas Sowell. *Marxism* (New York: William Morrow and Co., 1985), 210-211.

[9] James Thornton, "'Gramscian' Strategy at Work, *"The New American*, 18 September 1995, 25-26.

[10] W. Cleon Skousen. *The Naked Communist* (Salt Lake City: The Ensign Publishing Co., 1961), 259-263.

CHAPTER 6

TERRORISM: HOW SHOULD AMERICA RESPOND?

By Phil Fernandes

On September 11th, 2001, Islamic terrorists hijacked our planes and flew them into the Twin Towers and the Pentagon building. Brave Americans forced another hijacked plane to crash land in a wooded area of Pennsylvania. Thousands of Americans lost their lives. America was under attack.

If actions like this are to be prevented in the future, America must respond. This chapter deals with the steps we need to take, as a nation, to prevent terrorism in the future.

First, we must care for the sick, the suffering, and the dead (James 1:27). We must also comfort those who lost loved ones (Romans 12:15). However, helping the victims is just the beginning. We must punish the terrorists and protect our nation from future attacks.

Second, the United States government must identify and execute swift retribution on the terrorist organization and its leadership that are responsible for this atrocity (Romans 13:1-4). President Bush was right when he crushed the Al Qaida infrastructure and went after Osama bin Laden in Afghanistan. He is also right to continue to track down Al Qaida leaders around the world.

Third, the United States government must identify and punish governments known to encourage, fund, and/or shelter terrorists (or terrorist organizations) who have performed acts of terrorism against Americans. Countries like Saudi Arabia (most of the September 11 hijackers were from this country), Pakistan, and Iran (which now has provided shelter for one of bin Laden's sons and many of his Al Qaida leaders) must cooperate with the United States and turn over suspected terrorists linked to acts of violence against Americans.

Fourth, the United States government must continue to back the nation of Israel (Genesis 12:1-3). We must not allow Islamic terrorists to intimidate us into turning our backs on Israel, the chosen nation of God. Israel is our only true ally in the Middle East, and I believe that she is the closest friend that America has in this anti-American world.

Fifth, we must remind ourselves that the September 11th event does not have to mean the creation of a new world (or a "New World Order"). We don't need an international body to fight terrorism. Though cooperation with other nations is sometimes useful, the surrendering of United States sovereignty to an international body (like the United Nations) is simply not acceptable (Genesis 11; Revelation 13). Our biblically based constitution protects our God-given rights and freedoms; we should not expect the tyrannical governments that have good standing at the United Nations to protect us. Surrendering United States sovereignty would please the Osama bin Ladens of this violent world. It would not further the cause of peace.

Therefore, we must promote an intelligent patriotism, a patriotism that is pro-America, not pro-United Nations (Genesis 11; Revelation 13).

It seems to me that the current administration's infatuation with going to war with Iraq is more closely tied to United Nations interests than that of the United States. Enforcing UN resolutions should not be high on our priority list. Clearly there are countries with closer ties to Al Qaida than Iraq. Furthermore, if the United States government wants to invade Iraq for what we "think" she will do, then there should be a declaration of war by the United States Congress; it should not be a United Nations decision. According to the United States Constitution, only Congress can declare war.

Personally, I am opposed to military action that further strengthens the United Nations. I believe that the United Nations is a far greater threat to our freedom and security than Saddam Hussein will ever be. (The future antichrist is much more likely to come out of the United Nations, and the United Nations is a more likely candidate to rule the world than Hussein.) I also do not believe that either the United States or the United Nations has the right to police the nations of the world. The right to police the world implies the right to rule the world.

If America goes to war with Iraq, we should back our troops. They believe they are defending our freedom and they deserve our support. But building the New World Order through the United Nations is not worth the American blood that will be shed.

Sixth, our government should increase the efficiency of our intelligence operations without infringing on the freedoms of law-abiding citizens (Joshua 2). Our government should crack down on sedition and treason. The active promotion of the overthrow of our nation and its constitution was never protected by the first amendment (Matthew 12:17; Romans 13:1-7).

Still, the American people must not overreact; we must not surrender our freedoms (Genesis 1:27). We must refrain from asking our government officials to take away our freedoms in return for security. We must echo the sentiment of Patrick Henry who proclaimed "Give me liberty or give me death." Freedom is more important than security.

Also, the United States government must not overreact. Our government must not take excessive control over the lives of our citizens. In the opinion of this author, the Department of Homeland Security and the proposed Total Information Awareness program go a long way towards turning America into Big Brother, an all-knowing police state with the capability of tracking all electronic communications and transactions. Oregon Senator Ron Wyden has correctly labeled the TIA program "the most far-reaching government surveillance plan in history." We must remember that the terrorists hate this country because of our freedoms, and that to surrender these freedoms would serve the purposes of these terrorists.

Seventh, our government should protect our borders and stamp out illegal immigration. Any country that does not protect its borders is doomed to destruction. Our government officials should monitor closely non-citizens who come to this country from unfriendly, anti-American countries.

Eighth, we must also investigate our intelligence agencies to find out exactly what they knew concerning the hijackings prior to the attacks. If a people blindly trust their government and do not ask questions, that people will quickly lose their freedom. We now know that the FBI knew of at least one September 11th terrorist seeking flying instructions without wanting to learn how to take off or land a plane. No action was taken by the FBI. We also know of an FBI agent who is Muslim refusing to wear a microphone behind closed doors in an intelligence operation with suspected Islamic terrorists. At the very least, the FBI is guilty of negligence.

In short, we must defend our people and their freedoms. While we bring swift retribution on our attackers, we should not entangle ourselves with international bodies. This is America; we have a higher view of human life and rights than our European, post-Christian and often anti-American "brothers." Our founding fathers wanted to free us of the cancerous lust for power found in European circles. Now we seem focused on returning to the yoke of slavery. We must never allow tragedies like September 11th cause us to surrender our freedoms. Those who lost their lives on that infamous day died free. We fail to honor them if we choose to surrender the freedom that they enjoyed.

CHAPTER 7

THE IMPACT OF RELIGION ON GOVERNMENT

by Phil Fernandes

=================

Though we have all heard the liberal rallying cry of "separation of church and state," the fact of the matter is this: human government cannot exist in a spiritual vacuum. Human government must be based upon certain presuppositions about man and the universe in which he lives. In short, political and economic theories must be based upon a religious foundation. Thomas Jefferson, the author of *the Declaration of Independence*, recognized this when he penned the words, "all men are created equal." Even the atheists who signed the first *Humanist Manifesto* acknowledged man's reliance upon religious ideas by stating that, "nothing human is alien to the religious."[1] Human beings are incurably religious, and their governments must have a religious foundation as well.

THE JUDEO-CHRISTIAN WORLD VIEW

The United States government was founded upon the Judeo-Christian world view (i.e., the Bible).[2] Our founding fathers believed that all men were created equal and in God's image, and that all men have God-given rights that could not be taken away. God instituted human government to protect these unalienable rights.

According to our founding fathers, the need for human government is twofold. First, because man was created in God's image, human life is sacred and therefore worth protecting. Second, because man is in a fallen and sinful state, human life needs to be protected, for some humans infringe upon the God-given rights of other humans. Thus, the need for human government is based upon the biblical doctrines of Creation and the Fall.

Our founding fathers took seriously the sinfulness of mankind. They recognized that since human governments are ruled by sinful humans, government power must be limited. No man or group of men should be allowed to have their sinful lust for power go unchecked. Our nation's founders heeded Lord Acton's advice—"power corrupts, and absolute power corrupts absolutely." Therefore, *the Declaration of Independence* and the *United States Constitution* limited the power of government officials in several ways. First, God and His laws were recognized as existing above human government and its officials. Government officials are not above the law; they are answerable to God. Second, global government was rejected. A global government limited in power is an oxymoron. Third, a system of checks and balances and separation of powers (federal and state governments & the three branches of the federal government) were established to prevent the unleashing of a unified assault against the American people and their freedoms. Fourth, the people's rights to worship as they saw fit, elect many of their government officials, peacefully protest the government's actions, and bear arms were protected.

The Constitution does not force Americans to become Jews or Christians, but, because it is based upon the Judeo-Christian world view, it protects a person's freedom to worship according to the dictates of his or her conscience. The form of government America has and the freedoms we enjoy are due to the Judeo-Christian world view. Our founding fathers acknowledged the biblical view of government and morality in their political and economic thought. Political liberals may not like this fact, but it is a historical fact nonetheless. Although political liberals wish to change the religious presuppositions of our government, the alternatives are not very promising. And we must never forget that governments must have a religious base. We will now look at some of the alternatives to the Judeo-Christian basis for human government.

ATHEISM/SECULAR HUMANISM

In *Humanist Manifestos I and II*, atheist leaders proposed to save this planet by working towards a one-world socialistic government based upon the foundation of the atheistic world view.[3] However, in this century we have witnessed the horrors produced by governments based upon atheism. The totalitarian regimes of the Soviet Union and Red China together have systematically slaughtered more than 80 million of their own people in this century alone.[4]

Atheism, by denying belief in God's existence, is a world view that has no basis for the sanctity of human life. Man is merely molecules in motion, having no intrinsic worth. Since atheists also reject a historical Fall of mankind, man's lust for power is left unchecked. A survival of the fittest mentality is allowed to run rampant among government leaders. While claiming to have the best interests of the populace in mind, government officials are answerable to no one as they seek to increase their power.

Consistent atheism not only entails a rejection of traditional values, but also a complete denial of any absolute moral laws. Therefore, there is no such thing as right and wrong; the end (the goals of those in power) justifies the means (even if millions are slaughtered). Atheism fails to supply the moral foundation necessary for good government. Therefore, if the Judeo-Christian world view is rejected, we must look elsewhere for an alternative religious base for human government.

ISLAM

In the militant Islamic world view of Iran, the government leader (the ayatollah) is viewed as the infallible spokesman for God.[5] This is the Shi'ite branch of Islam. It perverts the Judeo-Christian world view by allowing a sinful man to stand in the place of God. The results can be the same as that of the atheistic world view since the atheist denial of God's existence causes its government leaders to attempt to replace God as the highest authority. The power of the government leader is not held in check. Whenever a human leader (other than the Lord Jesus who is fully God and fully man) stands in the place of God and claims to speak infallibly for God, oppression will almost surely follow. This was seen during the Carter administration when Ayatollah Khomeni took innocent Americans hostage for 444 days. The militant wing of Shi'ite Islam is known as Hezbollah.

The violent side of Islam is not only found in the Shi'ite Islam of Iran, but also in the Sunni Islam of other Muslim countries. Most Muslims in the world are Sunni Muslims. Within the Sunni branch of Islam, two movements deserve our attention. The Wahhabi movement originated in Saudi Arabia in the eighteenth century, and the Deobandi movement began in India in the nineteenth century and is currently popular in Pakistan.[6] Both branches of Sunni

Islam are reform movements within the Muslim world. These groups literally interpret the Koran (the Muslim holy book written by Muhammad) and the Hadith (early and authoritative Muslim traditions). Therefore, they take seriously Muhammad's commands to slay the idolaters or infidels (Surah 9:5; 5:34-35, etc.). They often use force and violence to purify the Islamic faith. This entails terrorist attacks on liberal or modern Muslims as well as acts of unprovoked violence against the non-Muslim world. The Al-Qaida terrorist network, the Taliban, and Osama Bin Laden have links with both Deobandi and Wahhabi Islam. The terrorist attacks against America on September 11, 2001 were the work of Bin Laden and his followers.

Though some would argue that violent Muslims, whether of the Shi'ite or Sunni type, are perverting the peaceful and tolerant religion of Islam, the facts tell a different story. Though most Muslims are probably peace-loving people, the Koran and the Hadith call for the slaying of non-Muslims wherever they are found. Muhammad meant Jihad (a holy war fought in the name of Allah, the Muslim God) to be taken literally; he himself conquered non-Muslims with the sword. In fact, whereas the first three centuries of Christianity saw thousands of defenseless Christians persecuted, the first three hundred years of Islam were characterized by Islamic military conquests of non-Muslim lands. Professing Christians who kill innocents in Jesus' name pervert the teachings of Christ; Muslims who commit terrorist acts in the name of Allah are following Muhammad's example and obeying the teachings of Muhammad as found in the Koran as well as the Hadith. A "back to the Bible" movement usually leads to religious freedom, while a "back to the Koran" movement will always lead to bloodshed and violence. It is no coincidence that every government heavily influenced by the Islamic faith offers no religious freedom to non-Muslims. In Middle-Eastern Muslim countries, non-Muslims can be executed for trying to convert a Muslim, and in the Sudan more than 2 million professing Christians have been killed by Muslims since the 1950's.

POLYTHEISM

Many tribal peoples in Africa and South America hold to the belief in many gods, called polytheism. The animism (the belief that all nature is animated with spirits) of American Indians was very similar to polytheism. History has shown that polytheism and animism leave their adherents in occultism, superstition, poverty, and anarchy. Human sacrifice is often practiced (i.e., Incas, Aztecs, Mayas). Polytheism offers no unified code of ethics to unite its people, since the gods are often opposed to one another. Ancient dictators were more than willing to bring in their own unifying principle (usually the enforced worship of the emperor or ruler as the superior god) while using polytheism to aid them in suppressing the rights of their people. In short, polytheism often produces a society that lacks a unified direction, thus making that society easy prey for potential dictators. The finite gods of polytheism are not able to sustain a society.

OTHER-WORLDLY PANTHEISM

Pantheism is the belief that God is the universe, and that, since man is part of the universe, man is God. In India, the society and government are based upon this world view due to India's most popular religion—Hinduism. But this type of Hindu pantheism in India is an *other-worldly* pantheism— the emphasis is not on this life, but on future reincarnations. This lessens the incentive of Hindus to alleviate the suffering of others, for the suffering person is working off negative karma. To alleviate his suffering would be to force him to return to this world, in a different body, and to suffer again to work off the negative karma. Thus, helping alleviate a person's sufferings is viewed as a hindrance to that person's spiritual progress. This is why many of the health care workers in India are Christian.

The caste system in India is another consequence of other-worldly pantheism. It is almost impossible for a person to leave the caste (or class) into which they are born, since the person is thought to be in that caste due to the karma he has brought from a former life. Usually, it is assumed that a future incarnation is the only way for a person to move out of their caste. Due to the other-worldly pantheism of India, suffering people are often neglected since they are thought to be working off negative karma.

It should be noted that any reform movements in India attempting to change the caste system are actually contrary to the doctrines of Hindu Pantheism. On the other hand, reform movements in America, such as the abolition of slavery, were actually bringing American life more in conformity to the Judeo-Christian world view.

THIS-WORLDLY PANTHEISM

In contrast to the other-worldly pantheism of India is the *this-worldly* pantheism of Nazi Germany.[7] In early twentieth century Germany the leadership of the German Church had all but apostacized. In earlier decades, German theologians and philosophers had attacked the authenticity and reliability of the Bible, causing many professing Christians in Germany to lose their confidence in the traditional Christian world view. The German Volk religion filled the void left by the church's apostacy. It became the dominating religious perspective of Germany's leadership.

The German Volk religion was a pantheistic ideology which held that the Aryan race is divine and that the German leader (Hitler) was the fullest manifestation of the divine. Non-aryan races were viewed as "sub-human." These races were seen as a threat to human progress, for it was feared that they could pollute the pure genetic make-up of the Aryan (master) race. The emphasis of the pantheism of the German Volk religion was on this life and the supposed future spiritual evolution of the Aryan race. The undesirable "sub-human" races had to be weeded out in order to usher in a "new age" of spiritual enlightenment.[8]

Thus, the holocaust, which took the lives of more than 6 million innocent Jews, was motivated by the this-worldly pantheism of Adolph Hitler and the Third Reich. The present-day version of this-worldly pantheism is the New Age Movement. Both the New Age Movement and the German Volk religion were greatly influenced by the occultic beliefs of Theosophy, a cult founded by the Russian mystic Helena Blavatsky.[9] The New Age Movement, if it continues to grow in popularity, may produce another holocaust; however, this holocaust may cover the entire earth. New Age leader and author Barbara Marx Hubbard believes that not everyone is ready for the coming New Age of peace and spiritual enlightenment. In fact, she believes that traditional Christians, Jews, and Muslims are holding back the spiritual evolution of mankind because they refuse to acknowledge that man is God. Therefore, reasons Hubbard, one-fourth of mankind needs to be exterminated in order to usher in the New Age.[10]

Pantheism (in both its this-worldly and other-worldly forms) teaches that God is an impersonal force, not the personal God of the Bible. Being an impersonal force, the God of pantheism is beyond the moral categories of right and wrong. Therefore, ultimately, there are no moral absolutes; what is right for one person is not necessarily right for another person, and visa versa. Usually this moral relativistic view translates into a toleration of willful, immoral behavior (i.e., homosexuality, abortion, euthanasia, sexual immorality, pornography, etc.), as well as an inconsistent lack of toleration of traditional values and beliefs (i.e., the Judeo-Christian world view). Unfortunately, that which a this-worldly pantheistic world view cannot tolerate it usually exterminates. For although the concept that man is God appears to be a high view of man, it is actually devalues human life since it entails the weeding out of undesirables who hold back human progress. (For the New Age Movement the undesirables include traditional Christians and Jews, as well as patriotic Americans who hold to traditional values.)

WHAT ABOUT THE INQUISITION AND THE CRUSADES?

Christianity is often blamed for the terrors of the Inquisition and the bloodshed of the Crusades. In reference to the Inquisition, several things need to be clarified. First, the Inquisition was primarily a killing & torturing of those who opposed the Bishop of Rome. In other words, it should not be viewed as an indictment on traditional, protestant Christianity (i.e., Bible-based Christianity). When the church and the Roman Empire merged, it was the empire that corrupted the church, not the other way around. Second, much of the inquisition dealt with torturing and killing Jews merely because they were Jews and they would not convert to "Christianity." But, true Christians cannot hate Jews. Jesus was Jewish. The apostles were Jewish. The Bible (Old and New Testaments) is Jewish. True Christians pray for Israel and love the Jewish nation since it is God's chosen nation. Jesus said "not everyone who says to Me 'Lord, Lord' shall enter the Kingdom of Heaven, but he who does the will of My Father in heaven" (Matthew 7:21). Third, Bible-believing Christians defend Jesus, not the actions of a fallible church. We do not believe the church is infallible, nor do we believe that the Bishop of Rome (i.e., the Pope) is infallible when he speaks for the entire church in areas of faith or practice. Protestants acknowledge that professing Christians have committed horrors in the name of Christ, but we believe that their actions prove them to be outside the true faith, for "faith without works is dead" (James 2:26). Fourth, during the Inquisition many true Christians were tortured and killed because they refused to submit to the Bishop of Rome. Often, the Inquisition was characterized by professing Christians killing true Bible-believing Christians as well as Jews.

The Crusades involved the waging of war in behalf of the Church of Rome. The early crusades were fought in defense of the Eastern Church as she was being attacked by Muslim invaders. Still, later Crusades morally deteriorated to the point where there is simply no way to justify them. Again, we must remember that these actions were ordered by the Roman Catholic Church. Protestants argue against the church hierarchy having that kind of authority; Protestants reject the notion of papal infallibility. Like the Inquisition, the Crusades show that not all professing believers are genuine Christians.

In a book entitled *Christianity on Trial*, authors Vincent Carroll and David Shiflett sum up the issue well:

> Whatever Christianity's role in the conflicts of the last two millennia, its hands were clean during the bloodiest century on record—the one just past. The body count from the two great barbarisms of the twentieth century, communism and Nazism, is extraordinary enough on its own. Communism's toll ran to perhaps 100 million . . . Adolph Hitler's death machine was equally efficient, but ran a much shorter course . . . Communism was and is proudly atheistic, while Nazism . . . embraced a form of neopaganism. Both were hostile to the organized religions in their midst, and neither genuflected before any power other than man himself. Yet these movements exterminated their

victims with an efficiency that clearly exceeded the most grisly achievement of states produced by Christian zealotry. In that sense, they were worthy heirs to the French Revolution, which erected altars to the Goddess of Reason before the backdrop of a guillotine.[11]

CONCLUSION

Government cannot be separated from religion. Every government must have a doctrine of man and his place in the universe, and it is here that government and religion overlap. If a government rejects the faith of our founding fathers (the Judeo-Christian world view), then it will accept an alternative world view. But the consequences of that alternative world view will infringe on man's freedom and eventually result in great loss of life, for the dethronement of God is not without consequences. Contemporary man's flight from God will inevitably lead him down the dark, bloody road to tyranny.

ENDNOTES

[1] Paul Kurtz, ed. *Humanist Manifesto I & II* (Buffalo: Prometheus Books, 1972), 9.

[2] It is true that not all of our founding fathers were Christians. Some were deists; they denied the miraculous elements of Christianity. Still, the founding fathers who were deists were *pro-Christian deists*. They were politically conservative and held to the biblical view of government and morality. On the other hand, *anti-Christian deists* could be found among the leaders of the bloody French Revolution. Anti-Christian deists are politically liberal—they believe that big government has all the answers to man's problems, and that man, through his reason, can save this planet. Anti-Christian deists reject the biblical view of limited government as well as the biblical view of morality. Modern deists usually fall into the anti-Christian deist camp. They often have more in common with secular humanists (i.e., atheists) than with adherents of the Judeo-Christian world view.

[3] Kurtz, 8, 10, 21.

[4] R. J. Rummel, *Death by Government* (New Brunswick: Transaction Publishers, 1994), 8.

[5] Timothy Demy and Gary P. Stewart, *In the Name of God* (Eugene: Harvest House Publishers, 2002), 58-59.

[6] Ibid., 59-62, 80-82.

[7] Richard Terrell, *Resurrecting the Third Reich* (Lafayette: Huntington House Publishers, 1994), 49-61, 145-168.

[8] Ibid., 50.

[9] Ibid., 49, 151-153.

[10] Tal Brooke, *One World* (Berkeley: End Run Publishing, 2000), 197. Hubbard is an insider with the United Nations and the United Religions Organization. She is not alone in her thinking. Her idea that a large portion of the world's population needs to be exterminated is shared by Cornell Professor David Pimentel. In 1994, he argued before the American Association for the Advancement of Science that the total population of the world should not exceed 2 billion people. Since the world's current population is about 6 billion, Pimentel apparently would like to see 4 billion people "disappear." Pimentel's wild idea was treated with respect by the *Los Angeles Times*. See William Norman Grigg, *Freedom on the Altar* (Appleton: American Opinion Publishers, 1995), 109.

[11] Vincent Carroll and David Shiflett, *Christianity on Trial* (San Francisco: Encounter Books, 2002), 109.

CHAPTER 8

THE NEW WORLD RELIGION

by Phil Fernandes

OVERVIEW OF THE SPIRITUAL HISTORY OF AMERICA

As Christianity continues to wane in America, as well as in the rest of Western civilization, a conscious movement to build a one-world religion is increasing in momentum and size. At its heart, this coming world religion is anti-Christian as it fosters worship of the earth and the revival of ancient pagan beliefs. To see how America has evolved from a Christian society into a neo-pagan culture, an overview of the spiritual history of America will be given.

Christian theism (1611-1960) dominated the thought of American culture from the arrival of the Pilgrims to the start of the 1960's. Christian theism held to the biblical view of God, morality, and religious freedom.

Several of our founding fathers (Thomas Jefferson, Ben Franklin, etc.) were deists. Deists were non-Christians who acknowledged God as Creator but rejected the biblical truth that God could intervene in human affairs through miracles. Deists also rejected the biblical teaching that Jesus is God. Still, our deistic founding fathers accepted the biblical view of government and morality. This is important since, although salvation of an individual necessitates trusting in the true Jesus of the Bible, the salvation and health of a nation is dependent upon acknowledgement of God's laws and obedience to those laws (Deuteronomy 28). Even the founding fathers that were deists acknowledged "the Laws of Nature and of Nature's God." This meant that they accepted God's moral laws written in our consciences as well as His moral laws found in the Bible.[1]

The Declaration of Independence acknowledged that "all men are created equal," and that God has given each human being "unalienable rights"—rights that human government cannot take away, rights that God instituted human government to protect. Our founding fathers believed that among these God-given rights were the rights to life, liberty, the pursuit of happiness, freedom of speech, freedom of religion, and the right to bear arms (the right to protect oneself).

The deists in America understood that Christian belief was healthy for the preservation of a society. The deists in France, to the contrary, were anti-Christian deists who attacked the Christian church with a vengeance. This led to the slaughter of many innocent people and government abuses of people's rights. This anti-Christian bias common among French deists marks the main difference between the American Revolution and the French Revolution.

The American nation got off to a great start as it based its views of government and morality on the Bible. Unprecedented prosperity followed as a result, and America quickly became the most powerful and wealthiest nation on earth.

However, the deist beliefs shared by some of our founding fathers did have a negative effect on American society. For if God does not or cannot intervene in the affairs of man, He is somewhat irrelevant in human history. This deistic downplaying of the relevance of God to a person's earthly life eventually opened the door to the atheistic belief that there is no God. For there exists only a small bridge between belief in an irrelevant God and the belief in no god (atheism). In short, deism is the "half-way house" between Christian theism and atheism. Deism aided the deterioration of the Christian influence on American society.

In 1859 Charles Darwin published his *Origin of Species*, in which he proposed a way of interpreting reality without acknowledging God as the Creator and Sustainer of the universe. Darwin argued for a natural (non-miraculous) origin of the universe, first life, and complex life forms. As the decades passed, his atheistic evolutionary ideology influenced many Americans, especially those in positions of leadership in government, education, media, and the churches. American society was gradually becoming more secular (non-religious).

In 1933 *Humanist Manifesto I* was drafted and signed by many influential atheists, including John Dewey, "the father of modern public education."[2] In this document, the signers proposed their plan to dethrone the already weakening Christian consensus in American society and to replace it with a secular humanistic (atheistic) belief system. The signers also argued for the need to bring about a one-world socialistic government. They expressed their belief that traditional religion (especially Christianity) is harmful, and that, through human reason and technology, man can save the planet. The signers of *Humanist Manifesto I* were influential enough to further the secularization of the government, schools, media, arts, and churches. Though most Americans retained a vague belief in God, they accepted, at least in practice, many of the assumptions of the secular humanists.

By 1960 secular humanism dominated much of the thought of American culture, especially in the media and the universities. This opened the floodgates for anti-Christian legislation and court decisions. Prayer and the Bible were removed from the public schools (1963), abortion was legalized (1973), and the homosexual rights movement began to gain momentum (1970's). Traditional religion and traditional morality were repeatedly slandered by the secular press, and moral relativism (the view that there are no moral absolutes; each person decides what is right or wrong for himself) became widespread.

When a government no longer acknowledges God as the ultimate authority, it begins to slowly replace God, believing itself to be the ultimate authority. It no longer conceives of its government officials as answerable to God. The government begins to play God by deciding which life is worth living. This is what happened in America. Laws were no longer based upon God's unchanging wisdom found in the Bible. Instead, laws became the arbitrary dictates of a governing elite that had replaced God. Human life was no longer held to be sacred since it was no longer thought to be created in God's image. (This explains how abortion, infanticide, and euthanasia came to be tolerated in America.) Without respect for God, the government began to see itself as an entity to be served by man, rather than as a God-ordained servant of man. Once God was removed from government policies, the government began to view itself as the all-sufficient provider—the answer to all of man's problems. This ultimately leads to the worship of the state. Keep in mind that this anti-God growth of government power began in the 1800's due to the influence of deism, well before secular humanism had achieved its complete victory in America by 1960.

However, as soon as secular humanism captured the reigns of American society, it began to loose its grip on those reigns. Secular humanism promised a meaningful, fulfilling life in a world without spiritual experiences. But, contrary to secular humanistic thinking, man cannot live on bread alone; man needs more than the physical things of this world; man has a spirit, and thus has spiritual needs. Atheism created a spiritual vacuum in America.

However, due to the fact that most Americans (though they retained some semblance of belief in God) rejected traditional Christianity, a return to Christianity was not considered a very popular option for American culture. Most Americans had accepted practical atheism. In other words, they lived like there is no God. Still, they rejected philosophical atheism (the belief there is no God). Therefore, they began to search for an alternative god that would not infringe upon their newly found moral autonomy. The God of the Bible was too demanding for most Americans.

The New Age Movement (a return to paganism) became the leading candidate for the new religion of America. As America searched for a new god to satisfy her hunger for spiritual experiences, she began to look to eastern religions such as Hinduism and Buddhism for answers. Soon, a new pantheistic religion was born on American soil.

Pantheism is the belief that god is an impersonal force rather than the personal God of the Bible. Pantheism teaches that the universe is god, and man, as part of the universe, is his own god, and that morality is relative to each person. New Age Pantheism entails the belief that man can save the planet by acknowledging his godhood and by uniting with all of mankind into a one-world government. This is often called "the Omega Point," and it will supposedly usher in an age of peace as man will have reached his final state of spiritual evolution.

A 1982 Gallup poll revealed that 23% of Americans believed in reincarnation (30% of 18-24 year olds believed in reincarnation), over 65% read astrology, and about 40% of Americans claimed to have had contact with the spirits of the dead. By the 1990's, New Age religion had dethroned secular humanism as the American religion.

THE THEOSOPHICAL CONNECTION

When one looks for the roots of pantheistic thinking in America, one must go back to 1875, when Helena Blavatsky founded the Theosophical Society.[3] The Theosophical Society promoted seances, spiritism (communication with the supposed spirits of the dead), and Hindu thought in the United States. This led to the current interest of many Americans in the New Age Movement (the return of ancient paganism).

The Theosophical Society has three primary goals. First, it seeks to declare the universal brotherhood of all mankind, culminating in a one-world government. Second, it focuses on teaching others the unity of all religions. Theosophists desire the development of a one-world, paganistic religion. Third, it encourages others to tap into the spiritual, occult powers latent within each person.

The Theosophical Society teaches that the world is awaiting many avatars (manifestations of God who reveal spiritual truth to the world). Blavatsky considered Jesus, Buddha, and Mohammed to be avatars. Of course, she reinterpreted Jesus' teachings and gave them a pantheistic, occultic slant.

After the death of Blavatsky, Annie Besant and Alice Bailey were later leaders of the Theosophical Society. Their books are still popular today within New Age circles. Bailey claimed to have communicated with several spirit guides. (Currently, this practice is known as channeling.) These spirit guides revealed to Bailey "the Plan," the steps to be taken in order to usher in the New Age and to bring to power the New Age Christ. Bailey's books are published through a company called "Lucius Trust," formerly known as the "Lucifer Publishing Company."[4]

It should be noted that Theosophy considers Lucifer the "enlightened one" whose wisdom will set mankind free. Satan's lie in the Garden of Eden—when he told Eve that if she ate from the forbidden fruit she would be as God—is viewed not as a lie by Theosophy, but as the ultimate truth that, once accepted by the human race as a whole, will usher in the New Age. Blavatsky's 1888 work entitled *The Secret Doctrine* states that Lucifer is higher and older than the God of the Bible, and that Satan and his hosts are the "Lords of Wisdom." In fact, Blavatsky once published a monthly journal called *Lucifer*. Hence, at its core, Theosophy entails the worship of Satan.[5]

Thus, a case can be made that the Theosophical Society is the root or origin of the New Age Movement in America. But, it should also be considered one of the current driving forces of New Age thought, as well as the ultimate destination of the New Age Movement. Many of the New Agers who are fighting for a one-world religion, and have great influence on the United Nations, also have Theosophical connections. The Lucius Trust, a creation of the Theosophical Society, maintains the meditation room in the UN headquarters.[6] Robert Muller, former Assistant Secretary-General of the UN, has been greatly influenced in his religious and political thought by the writings of theosophist Alice Bailey. Muller still exerts much influence on the UN in areas of education and religion.[7] UN favorites Mikhail Gorbachev and Maurice Strong also have Theosophical leanings.[8] Indeed, it would not be far from the mark to identify the religion of the United Nations with Theosophy.

NEW AGE THINKERS AND LEADERS

Besides the leaders of the Theosophical cult, there were and are many other neo-pagan thinkers who have led or are leading many people into the New Age movement. A few of these thinkers and leaders are mentioned below.

Carl G. Jung (1875-1961) was a psychologist and disciple of the atheist Sigmund Freud. Jung broke with Freud's atheism due to Jung's mystical and pantheistic (his view of the collective unconscious) ideas. Jung helped to evolve secular psychology into more of a paganistic, New Age version. The popularity of New Age psychology helped prepare Americans for the New Age religion.[9]

Pierre Teilhard de Chardin (1881-1955) was a heretical Jesuit priest and Roman Catholic. His lifelong goal was to merge the physical and spiritual worlds through evolutionary science. Chardin was a pantheist (though he refused to admit this) since he taught that man and the earth were divine. He taught that Christ is "the Omega Point," the final stage of human evolution.[10] Chardin may be the most widely read New Age author today. He has influenced many powerful people, including former Vice President Al Gore, former Assistant Secretary-General of the United Nations Robert Muller, and Trilateralist Zbigniew Brzezinski.

Edgar Cayce (1877-1945) was a false prophet who would make predictions and medical diagnosis while in trance states. Known as the "sleeping prophet," he was the forerunner of many modern day channelers. He was a pantheist who believed in reincarnation and rejected traditional Christianity.[11] The Association for Research and Enlightenment continues to proclaim his teachings to many New Agers today.

Benjamin Creme is a British Theosophist who has been proclaiming the coming of a New Age messiah called "Lord Maitreya" since 1982. Lord Maitreya belongs to the Spiritual Hierarchy called the Ascended Masters. Supposedly,

Maitreya appears periodically to aid mankind in his spiritual evolution. The evidence for the reality of Lord Maitreya is non-existent, but, according to Creme, this is due to the fact that Maitreya will not manifest himself to mankind until we are spiritually ready.[12] Barbara Marx Hubbard is a New Ager who has been an advisor to the US Senate and House of Representatives, and currently speaks at many United Nations gatherings. She is calling for the extermination of up to one-fourth the world's population—adherents of traditional Christianity, Judaism, and Islam—because they refuse to acknowledge they are god, thus blocking progress towards the New Age.[13]

Robert Muller, former Assistant Secretary-General of the United Nations, is the author of *The World Core Curriculum*, a document that has earned him the title "the father of global education." *The World Core Curriculum* promotes globalism and New Age beliefs, and is an attempt to set forth the principles for the education programs of all nations. This curriculum, which attempts to convert students into "global citizens," received a warm welcome at the United Nations and is now being implemented in many nations. Muller's *The World Core Curriculum* is making inroads into American public education and was the driving force behind the Goals 2000 campaign in American schools. Muller acknowledges that his thought has been greatly inspired by Theosophy's Alice Bailey and New Ager Pierre Teilhard de Chardin.[14]

At the 1993 Parliament of World Religions, Muller was the keynote speaker. During his speech, he called for the creation of an organization dedicated to promoting religious unity in the world. Muller envisioned a "United Religions" as a sister organization to the United Nations. Through "the United Religions Initiative," this is becoming a reality. Over 5,000 religious leaders attended the Parliament. Besides leaders of traditional religions, many of the participants represented newer occultic religions.[15]

Maurice Strong, Canadian billionaire and New Age globalist, served as the chairman of the UN sanctioned "Earth Summit" in 1992. There, he and Mikhail Gorbachev were selected by the UN to produce an "Earth Charter," a list of international regulations to govern human behavior in areas concerning the environment. New Age pantheistic assumptions (earth worship, the oneness of all reality, etc.) and environmental pseudo-science saturated both the Earth Summit and the Earth Charter.[16]

Former Soviet dictator Mikhail Gorbachev is now preaching a New Age/worship the earth message. He promotes radical environmentalism through his Green Cross organization, and authored the "Earth Charter" mentioned above.[17]

The Gorbachev Foundation sponsored the 1995 "State of the World Forum," held in San Francisco. The forum was titled "Toward a New Civilization: Launching a Global Initiative." Attending the forum were globalists from the Trilateral Commission, the Council on Foreign Relations, the Club of Rome, the Bilderbergers; key political personalities such as former President Bush, Margaret Thatcher, former Secretaries of State James Baker and George Schultz, Zbigniew Brzezinski, as well as other former and current leaders from around the globe. But also present at the forum were leading New Agers such as Barbara Marx Hubbard, Fritjof Capra, Deepak Chopra, Robert Muller, Matthew Fox, Maurice Strong, Shirley MacLaine, and Ted Turner.

During Gorbachev's keynote address at the forum, he proposed the establishment of a "United Nations Council of Elders," a group of "intellectuals" who would set out to solve the world's greatest problems. Gorbachev also spoke of "spiritual renewal" on a global scale and the ushering in of "the next phase of human development," both New Age themes.[18] It appears that Gorbachev is a key player in uniting political globalists and New Age globalists to form a powerful coalition that will produce both the New World

Order and the New World Religion.

DOCTRINES OF THE COMING NEW WORLD RELIGION

Since the New Age movement is not one unified organization, but instead a network of many different organizations that share neo-pagan and occultic beliefs and practices, there is no one set of doctrines to which all New Agers unanimously agree. Still, there is enough common ground between New Agers for one to identify a set of doctrines adhered to by most New Agers.[19] Below is a list of some of the more common New Age beliefs. From this list, it will become evident that the New Age movement is not compatible with biblical Christianity.

Pantheism is the belief that all reality is ultimately one being. This one being is the universe, and the universe is god. God is an impersonal force, not the personal God of Christianity. Since man is part of the universe, man is god. On the other hand, Christianity teaches that God is a personal God who created the universe out of nothing (Genesis 1:1). Therefore, God cannot be equated with the universe.

Because New Agers are pantheists, they worship the earth. The earth is often personalized by New Agers as Gaia, the earth goddess. This is especially true in Wicca (modern witchcraft), where earth worship and radical feminism are merging. Due to New Age worship of the earth, New Agers are often involved in fanatical environmental activism based on faulty science. The Bible is unambiguous in its assertion that the Creator is not to be identified with His creation, and that we are to worship the Creator, not the creation (Romans 1:18-25).

Pluralism is the belief that all religions lead to god, and that ultimately all religions teach the same truths. Therefore, all religions should be merged into one unified global religion. The Bible, on the other hand, teaches that salvation comes only through Jesus who died on the cross for our sins and rose from the dead to conquer death for us. Only Christianity is the true religion; all other religions are false (John 14:6; 1 Peter 2:24; 3:18).

Since New Agers are moral relativists, they believe there is no such thing as sin. Since they reject the reality of sin, man does not need to be saved; he only needs to acknowledge his own deity, thus escaping the spiritual ignorance that blinds him. The Bible says that man is not God; he is a sinner who needs to be saved by God's grace through Jesus (Romans 3:23; 6:23; Ephesians 2:8-9).

Instead of the biblical doctrine of salvation through faith in Jesus, New Agers believe in reincarnation. Reincarnation is the doctrine that the individual soul passes through the cycle of death and rebirth, and that the soul reanimates a different body (whether animal or human) after death until all negative karma is done away with. Then the individual soul is absorbed into the world soul. The Bible clearly disagrees by stating that, " it is appointed for man to die once and then comes the judgment" (Hebrews 9:27).

New Agers deny the existence of absolute truth. Therefore, they proclaim that all beliefs are equally true and that they are opposed to all forms of dogmaticism (the acceptance of absolute truths). However, the New Age belief that there is no absolute truth is self-refuting, since the only way this belief could be true is if it is an absolute truth. New Agers are very dogmatic in their rejection of dogmaticism; they are very intolerant of everyone who rejects their supposedly absolute "tolerance."

New Agers believe they can receive wisdom and power from the spirit realm. Therefore, they try to commune with this realm through various practices. Through channeling, New Agers allow their bodies to be possessed by spirit entities that speak through them, revealing spiritual "truth." The Bible condemns channeling as voluntary demonic possession

(Isaiah 8:19; Deuteronomy 18:9-12; 29:29). Since the dead cannot communicate with the living (Luke 16:19-31), the spirit entities that possess channelers are not the spirits of deceased humans. Rather, they are demons (fallen, evil angels) who deceive humans. The scriptures command us to test the spirits, for not every spirit is from God (1 John 4:1-3). The Apostle Paul warned us that, in the last days, men will fall prey to doctrines taught by demons (1 Timothy 4:1). The content of channeled messages contradicts the Gospel message and must be rejected (Galatians 1:8-9).

New Agers often attempt to be at one with the divine through eastern meditation. During this practice, the New Ager surrenders the control of his mind by emptying his mind through the cessation of rational thought. This leaves a person vulnerable to demon possession. Mantras are often repeated during New Age meditation. A mantra is a one syllable word that, when repeated over and over, is designed to remove all content from the mind. This practice is in direct disobedience to the teaching of Christ, who prohibited His followers from engaging in the vain repetition which was common among pagan worshipers (Matthew 6:7). The mantras have been shown to have been derived from the names of Hindu deities (false gods).[20] Therefore, eastern meditation invites demon possession through the emptying of one's mind and the communion with false gods (1 Corinthians 10:19-21). In biblical meditation, a Christian focuses his mind on truths from God's Word (Psalm 1:1-2; Joshua 1:8). Therefore, in biblical meditation, the mind is never left empty.

New Agers reject the true Jesus of the Bible by denying that Jesus is uniquely God and the only Savior of mankind (John 14:6). They deny that He died on the cross as the substitute sacrifice for our sins and that He rose from the dead to conquer death for us (1 Peter 2:24; 3:18; Matthew 28; Luke 24; John 20; 21).

New Agers believe that man himself can bring about

world peace; they do not trust in Jesus as the only the Prince of Peace (Isaiah 9:6).

All New Agers believe in the coming New Age of peace and spiritual enlightenment. Once all of mankind recognizes the divinity of each person the final stage in man's spiritual evolution will have arrived. At this point, the planet will be saved.

Many New Agers await the coming of a New Age Christ or Messiah, someone who will save the planet by leading mankind into the New Age of peace and enlightenment. If such a person were to come to power, the Bible would classify him as a false messiah and a leading candidate for either the antichrist or the false prophet (the demon-possessed rulers who will deceive and enslave mankind shortly before the return of Jesus, the true Messiah).

THE UNITED RELIGIONS INITIATIVE

Robert Muller (Chancellor of the UN Peace University), Juliet Hollister (founder of the theosophical Temple of Understanding), and Episcopal Bishop William Swing drafted the "United Religions Initiative" in 1996. Bishop Swing has become the initiative's leading spokesperson. Through this initiative, Swing hopes to unite the religions of the world into one body, "the United Religions Organization." Swing's goals are to have the initiative signed by 60 million people and for the United Religions Organization to be up and running by the year 2005.[21]

A one-world demonic religion is being created in our midst. Christians must be willing to oppose and expose the work of Satan in our age. We must follow the example of the true believers who lived in Germany as the Nazis were coming to power: they spoke out against the evils of the Third Reich and did whatever they could to combat the Nazi atrocities. Bible believers must proclaim God's truth and stand against the evil new world religion.

ENDNOTES

[1] Herbert W. Titus, *The Declaration of Independence: The Christian Legacy* (Chesapeake: Titus Publications, 1995), 6-9.

[2] Paul Kurtz, ed., *Humanist Manifestos I and II* (Amherst: Prometheus Books, 1933 & 1973).

[3] Walter Martin, *Kingdom of the Cults* (Minneapolis: Bethany House Publishers, 1985), 246-260.

[4] William Norman Grigg, *Freedom on the Altar* (Appleton: American Opinion Publishing, 1995), 165.

[5] Ibid.

[6] Ibid., 159.

[7] Gary H. Kah, *The New World Religion* (Noblesville, Indiana: Hope International Publishing, 1998), 175, 171-172.

[8] Grigg, 174-175.

[9] Kah, 54-62. See also Tal Brooke, *One World* (Berkeley: End Run Publishing, 2000), 33-35.

[10] Ibid., 62-70. See also Tal Brooke, 188-189.

[11] Kah, 74-91.

[12] Grigg, 161-162.

[13] William F. Jasper, "Global Gorby," *New American*, 30 October 1995, 28-29.

[14] Kah, 171-178.

[15] Ibid., 209-212.

[16] Grigg, 174-176.

[17] Ibid.

[18] Jasper, 23-29.

[19] Brooke, 57-60.

[20] Elliot Miller, *A Crash Course on the New Age Movement* (Grand Rapids: Baker Book House, 1989), 94.

[21] Brooke, 189-192. See also Kah, 216-219.

CHAPTER 9

GOVERNMENT AND OLD TESTAMENT LAW

by Phil Fernandes

THEONOMY

Theonomy is a school of thought within evangelicalism that believes that Gentile governments should enforce the Law of Moses (the Old Testament Law) just as ancient Israel did. Theonomy means "God's law." Theonomists are also called reconstructionists because they want to reestablish the Law of Moses in the governments of the nations of this world. This school of thought is often referred to as dominion theology since theonomists believe that God has called the church to take dominion over the earth; the church is to rule the state.

Theonomists believe that the Mosaic Law has three aspects: the ceremonial, the moral, and the civil. Theonomists acknowledge that the ceremonial law was fulfilled by Christ and no longer applies today. Therefore, they do not adhere to the Old Testament dietary laws, nor do they desire to build a temple and reinstitute animal sacrifices. The ceremonial law pointed forward to Christ. Now that Jesus has come, we are no longer under the ceremonial law.

On the other hand, theonomists believe that the moral and civil aspects of the Mosaic Law still apply today. The moral law deals with God's absolute, unchanging moral laws (such as thou shalt not kill, thou shalt not steal, thou shalt not commit adultery, etc.), and these are still in effect.

The civil aspects of the Mosaic Law dealt with the list of punishments for crimes found in the Pentateuch (the books of Moses; the first five books of the Bible). The list of crimes and punishments that God gave to the nation of Israel, according to theonomists, also should be enforced by Gentile governments today. This would mean that sins like idolatry and adultery would require the death penalty for the guilty parties.

Theonomists believe that every Old Testament Law is still binding today unless God specifically removed that particular law in the New Testament. As discussed, theonomists acknowledge that the New Testament teaches that Christ fulfilled the Old Testament ceremonial laws; therefore, these laws are no longer in effect today. However, theonomists argue that since God did not abrogate or lay aside the moral or civil laws in the New Testament, they are still in effect today.

Most theonomists are postmillennialists; they believe that the Gospel will be accepted throughout the world until the church will reign over the earth and usher in a long age of peace and righteousness. After this extended period of time, Jesus will return to judge the living and the dead.

Most theonomists believe that the church has replaced Israel, and that the present nation of Israel is not really God's chosen nation. Only the church, in their view, is God's chosen people. Hence, theonomists are not looking for a future revival in Israel in which the Jews accept Jesus as their Savior and Messiah.

DISPENSATIONALISM

Dispensationalists form another school of thought within evangelicalism. Dispensationalists disagree with theonomists concerning the application of the Mosaic Law to Gentile governments. Dispensationalists believe that the Mosaic Law cannot be broken down into different aspects, such as the moral, ceremonial, and civil aspects. Dispensationalists teach that the entire Mosaic Law must be accepted as a whole or laid aside as a whole. The dispensationalist believes that we are no longer under the Law of Moses; we are now under the Law of Christ. By this, they mean that only those Old Testament Laws that are repeated and reaffirmed in the New Testament still apply today.

Dispensationalists are premillennialists—they believe that Jesus will return before the age of peace begins and that He will literally reign upon the earth for 1,000 years. They reject the theonomist notion that the church will reign on the earth before Jesus returns. Dispensationalists teach that the church will only reign upon the earth after Jesus returns, and then the church will reign with Jesus.

Dispensationalists also believe that God is not through with the nation of Israel—she is still the chosen nation of God. According to dispensational theology, a day will come when all Israel will acknowledge Jesus as Savior and Messiah. At that point, Jesus will return to rescue Israel from her enemies. Jesus will then establish Israel as the greatest nation on earth, and He will reign over the entire world from the rebuilt temple in Jerusalem.

MY VIEW

I do not agree wholeheartedly with either the theonomist or the dispensationalist. I believe that both extremes are mistaken, and that the truth lies somewhere between these two positions.

First, I accept the dispensational view called premillennialism (although I reject the pretribulational rapture; I am a posttribulationalist). I believe that the Bible clearly teaches that Jesus will return before the age of peace and righteousness and that He, with His church, will literally reign over the entire earth for 1,000 years (Revelation 20).

Second, I reject the theonomist idea that the church has replaced Israel. Israel is still God's chosen nation, and she does have a future in God's prophetic timetable. The day will come when all Israel will acknowledge Jesus as Savior and Messiah, and all Israel will be saved (Romans 11:25-27).

Third, I reject the dispensationalist contention that the Mosaic Law cannot be subdivided into three aspects: moral, ceremonial, and civil. I agree with the theonomist on this point. I believe distinctions can be made between the moral, ceremonial, and civil aspects of the Mosaic Law.

Fourth, though I agree with the theonomist that the moral aspect of the Mosaic Law is still binding today, I disagree with theonomy concerning the civil law. The civil law was prescribed by God specifically for Israel in her historical situation. It may or may not be a good idea to apply a certain Old Testament civil law to Gentile governments today. Each law must be dealt with on a case by case basis.

For example, I do not believe that idolaters, adulterers, or rebellious sons should be put to death today for those offenses (Exodus 22:18, 20; Deuteronomy 22:22; 21:18-21). God often dealt with Israel in a harsh, strict manner, for she, as God's chosen nation, was entrusted with God's revelation in written form. God often had to go to "extremes" to keep her religion pure and undefiled so that God's revelation would not be corrupted. God had blessed Israel more abundantly than any other nation, but, with added blessings came more responsibility.

Some Old Testament Laws were more lenient than our laws should be today. For instance, I think that a more severe penalty for rape is called for in today's society. In ancient times, God's Old Testament Law greatly increased woman's rights, but God apparently did not intend to make all the necessary changes at once. Today, a rapist should be punished harshly, not forced to marry his victim if she is a non-betrothed virgin (Deuteronomy 22:28-29).

The Israelites were a nomadic people; hence, they could not imprison criminals. We have that option today. Therefore, there are some cases in which capital punishment was required in the Old Testament, but a long prison term might suffice today. Of course, the death penalty for premeditated murder should continue to be enforced, for the punishment must fit the crime.

Finally, I agree with both theonomists and dispensationalists that the ceremonial law was fulfilled by Christ. Neither camp argues that Gentiles should reinstitute animal sacrifices and adhere to ancient Jewish dietary laws.

I believe that both schools of thought have oversimplified the issues involved. We do not have to simply see if the New Testament repeats an Old Testament law to know that it is still in effect today (dispensationalism). Nor, should we assume that all Old Testament laws still apply today unless they are clearly removed in the New Testament. When it comes to the civil aspects of the Mosaic Law, the issue is less obvious then either the dispensationalist or the theonomist would have us believe.

In short, the ceremonial laws were fulfilled by Jesus; they no longer apply today. The moral laws are God's eternal, unchanging moral laws; they will never be removed. All governments should base their laws upon God's unchanging moral principles. But, Israel's civil laws should be dealt with on a case by case basis.

I believe the founding fathers were correct in acknowledging freedom of religion, rather than choosing to execute non-believers (as required by the Mosaic Law). They were right to refrain from trying to replace Israel by instituting the civil aspects of the Mosaic Law across the boards. We can gain much insight from studying the civil aspects of the Mosaic Law, but that does not mean that it is God's will for Gentile nations to enforce these civil laws in exactly the same manner as Israel.

CHAPTER 10

AMERICA AND THE FALL OF ROME

by Phil Fernandes

E very generation has its prophet. It appears that our prophet was the great Christian thinker, Francis Schaeffer (1912-1984). Like the prophets of Israel, he called his nation to repent of her wicked ways. But, like Israel, America has yet to turn from her sin.

Schaeffer was a man who saw America following in the footsteps of the ancient Roman Empire. In his book *How Should We Then Live?*, Schaeffer traced the steps that Rome took in her decline. Schaeffer noted that Rome tried to build her society on the limited gods she worshiped. However, these gods were too small to sustain an empire and protect the freedoms of men. These gods were not true divinity; they were merely amplified humanity. Schaeffer believed that only the unlimited God of the Bible could sustain a government while protecting the freedoms of men. Without the unlimited God of the Bible and His unchanging moral laws, citizens of Rome were at the mercy of the arbitrary decisions of their human leaders. Without the infinite God of the Bible as the foundation of a society, that society can move in only two directions: anarchy or tyranny. Without God's absolute moral laws, the selfish desires of men began to dominate the legal thought of Rome. Sexual immorality and violence began to become more and more common in Roman culture. Armed gangs roamed the streets. Finally, fear was so widespread that the citizens of Rome practically begged their leaders for an authoritative government. The people of Rome were willing to surrender their freedoms in exchange for more protection from the government. The people failed to realize that the government could also do them harm. Once the government had complete control over their lives, if the government chose to suppress its people, there would be no earthly place left for them to turn for protection.

Schaeffer saw parallels between the decline of Roman freedom and the trends in America during our generation. Though Schaeffer died more than a decade ago, he was able to foresee our country traveling down the same path as the Roman Empire. The sexual promiscuity and moral laxity of the 1960's has led to the gang violence of the 1990's. After several major terrorist bombings and attacks (i.e., Oklahoma City, the twin towers, the Pentagon), American citizens are pleading with our government to take away our freedoms in return for an increase in government "protection." Freedoms that were once considered sacred by our founding fathers are now in jeopardy of being given away. American citizens seem willing to blindly trust the government and surrender their freedom to speak out against the government and their right to bear arms. Americans have forgotten the lesson learned by our founding fathers: the greatest enemy to be feared is often the government itself.

The answer for America is not more government

control. The only solution is a return to the unchanging moral laws of the infinite God of the Bible. There are only two options. America must either return to its former standing as "one nation under God," or America will follow the path taken by Rome and become one nation under an authoritative regime. Our nation must heed the warning of its prophet. Francis Schaeffer may have been "a voice crying in the wilderness." But, if one listens closely, one can still hear the echo of his voice.

CHAPTER 11

THE DEATH OF MAN: THE COMING DEATH OF WESTERN CIVILIZATION

by Phil Fernandes

═══════════════════════════════

As the twentieth century comes to a close, we must properly diagnose the disease that has caused the unprecedented wars, bloodshed, and genocide which this century has experienced. In this paper I will discuss the prophetic insights of the German atheist Friedrich Nietzsche, as well as the prognostication of Christian thinkers C. S. Lewis and Francis Schaeffer, concerning the future of Western civilization. I will show that the nineteenth century's death of God has led to the twentieth century's death of both universal truth and absolute moral values, and that this in turn will lead to the death of man in the twenty-first century if the tide is not reversed.

NIETZSCHE: PROPHET FOR THE 20TH CENTURY

Friedrich Nietzsche (1844-1900) proclaimed that "God is dead."[1] By this he meant that the Christian world view was no longer the dominant influence on the thought of Western culture. Nietzsche reasoned that mankind had once created God through wishful thinking, but the nineteenth century man intellectually matured to the point where he rejected God's existence.[2] Intellectuals throughout the world were embracing atheism as their world view, and the ideas of these intellectuals were beginning to influence the common people throughout Western civilization. According to Nietzsche, scientific and technological advances had made belief in God untenable.

But Nietzsche saw a contradiction in the thought of these intellectuals. Though he agreed with their atheism, he rejected their acceptance of traditional moral values. Nietzsche argued that, since God is dead, traditional values have died with Him.[3] If the God of the Bible does not exist, reasoned Nietzsche, then the moral values taught in the Bible should have no hold over mankind.

Nietzsche viewed existence as a struggle and redefined the good as "the will to power."[4] This was a logical outgrowth of his acceptance of the Darwinian doctrine of the survival of the fittest. Nietzsche called for a group of "supermen" to arise with the boldness to create their own values.[5] He proposed that, through their will to power, these "supermen" replace the "soft values" of Christianity with what he called "hard values." Nietzsche believed that the "soft values" of Christianity (self-control, sympathy, love for enemies, human equality, mercy, humility, dependence on God, etc.) were stifling human creativity and progress; these values encouraged mediocrity. But the "hard values" of the supermen (self-assertion, daring creativity, passion, total independence, desire for conquest, etc.) greatly enhance creativity.[6] Nietzsche considered the soft values a slave morality, and the hard values a master morality, and he promoted the latter.

Nietzsche rejected the idea of universal, unchanging truths. He viewed truths as mere human creations, as metaphors mistaken for objective reality.[7] Therefore, Nietzsche showed that, since God is dead, universal truth, like absolute moral values, is dead as well.

Nietzsche predicted that the twentieth century man would come of age. By this he meant that the atheist of the twentieth century would realize the consequences of living in a world without God, for without God there are no absolute moral values. Man is free to play God and create his own morality. Because of this, prophesied Nietzsche, the twentieth century would be the bloodiest century in human history.[8] Still, Nietzsche was optimistic, for man could create his own meaning, truth, and morality. Set free from belief in a non-existent God, man could excel like never before. Nietzsche viewed the changes that would occur as man becoming more than man (the superman or overman), rather than man becoming less than man.

Nietzsche was the forerunner of postmodernism. A key aspect of modernism was its confidence that, through reason, man could find absolute truth and morality. Postmodernism rejects this confidence in human reason. All claims to having found absolute truth and morality are viewed by postmodernists as mere creations of the human mind.[9]

The history of the twentieth century has proven Nietzsche's basic thesis correct. Western culture's abandonment of the Christian world view has led to a denial of both universal truth and absolute moral values. The twentieth century has proven to be the bloodiest century in human history.[10] Hence, the Christian thinker must object to the optimism of Nietzsche. The death of God is not a step forward for man; it is a step backward—a dangerous step backward. If God is dead, then man is dead as well.

The comments of Roman Catholic philosopher Peter Kreeft are worth noting:

> One need not share Nietzsche's atheism to agree with his historical, not theological, dictum that "God is dead"—i.e., that faith in God is dead as a functional center for Western civilization, that we are now a planet detached from its sun. One need not share Nietzsche's refusal of morality and natural law to agree with his observation that Western man is increasingly denying morality and natural law; that we are well on our way to the Brave New World.[11]

C. S. LEWIS: THE ABOLITION OF MAN

The nineteenth century brought the death of God to Western culture. The twentieth century brought the death of truth and morality to Western culture. Two twentieth century Christian thinkers, C. S. Lewis (1898-1963) and Francis Schaeffer (1912-1984), argued that the death of man will follow, unless of course man repents.

A Christian thinker should not be content with rightly analyzing and critiquing current ideas. A true thinker should also attempt to foresee the probable future consequences of ideas. In this way, a Christian thinker performs the role of a watchman by warning his listeners of future dangers (Ezekiel 33:1-9). C. S. Lewis and Francis Schaeffer had the courage to fulfill this role.

Lewis, in his prophetic work *The Abolition of Man*, critiqued an English textbook, written in the 1940's, which was designed for school children. Lewis found that more than English was being taught in this book, for the authors rejected objective truth and traditional values and proclaimed a type of moral relativism.[12] Lewis expressed concern for two reasons. First, the children who read this textbook would be easy prey to its false teachings.[13] Second, this would lead to a culture built on moral relativism and the rejection of objective truth, something that, according to Lewis, has not existed in the history of mankind.[14]

Lewis not only refuted the fallacious views of the authors, but also predicted the future consequences of this type of education. He argued that teaching of this sort would produce a race of "men without chests."[15] By this he meant men without consciences. According to Lewis, this would mean an entirely "new species" of man and "the abolition of man."[16]

Lewis argued that the practical result of such education would be "the destruction of the society which accepts it."[17] The rejection of all values leaves man free to recreate himself and his values.[18] When this power is placed into the hands of those who rule, their subjects will be totally at their mercy.

Lewis also saw in this rejection of traditional values a new purpose for science. In a sense, science is like magic in that both science and magic represent man's attempted "conquest of nature." However, science will become an instrument through which a few hundreds of men will rule billions of men,[19] for in man's conquest of nature, human nature will be the last aspect of nature to surrender to man.[20] Science will be used by future rulers to suppress the freedoms of the masses.

Lewis refers to the future rulers as "the man-moulders of the new age" or the "Conditioners."[21] It will be the job of the Conditioners to produce the rules, not to obey the rules.[22] The Conditioners (i.e., Nietzsche's supermen) will boldly create the laws the conditioned must obey. The role of education will become the production of artificial values which will serve the purposes of the Conditioners.[23] The Conditioners, through their Nietzschean "will to power" and motivated by the thirst to satisfy their own desires, will create their own new values and then force these "values" on the masses.[24]

According to Lewis, the rejection of traditional values and objective truth will lead to the same mentality in future rulers as that of "the Nazi rulers of Germany."[25] Traditional values will be replaced by the arbitrary wills of the few who rule over the billions,[26] and this will "abolish man" and bring about "the world of post-humanity."[27]

SCHAEFFER: THE POST-CHRISTIAN ERA & THE DEATH OF MAN

Francis Schaeffer proclaimed that Western culture is now in a "post-Christian era." By this he meant the same thing Nietzsche meant when he declared "God is dead." Schaeffer was saying that the Christian world view was no longer the dominant presupposition of Western culture. Now, a secular humanistic view of reality permeates the thought of the West.[28] Due to this change in world view, modern man has fallen below what Schaeffer called "the line of despair."[29] Schaeffer meant that, by throwing the God of the Bible out of the equation, modern man, left to himself and without divine revelation, could not find absolute truth and eventually gave up his search for it. According to Schaeffer, modern man no longer thinks in terms of antithesis (i.e., the law of non-contradiction); he now views truth as relative. And, since he believes there are no absolutes, modern man has rejected universal moral laws and has embraced moral relativism.

Schaeffer wrote concerning America, "our society now functions with no fixed ethics," and "a small group of people decide arbitrarily what, from their viewpoint, is for the good of society at that precise moment and they make it law."[30] Schaeffer compares this present climate of arbitrary lawmaking to the fall of the Roman Empire. The finite gods of Rome where not sufficient to give a base in law for moral absolutes; therefore, the Roman laws were lax and promoted self-interest rather than social harmony. This eventually led to a state of social anarchy as violence and promiscuity spread throughout the empire. To keep order, the Roman Empire had to become increasingly more authoritative. Due to Rome's oppressive control over its people, few Romans believed their culture was worth saving when the barbarian invasions began.[31] Schaeffer saw that America, like ancient Rome, had turned to arbitrary laws which have led to an increase in crime and promiscuity, which in turn has led to ever-increasing government control. Schaeffer stated this principle as follows:

> The humanists push for "freedom," but having no Christian consensus to contain it, that "freedom" leads to chaos or to slavery under the state (or under an elite). Humanism, with its lack of any final base for values or law, always leads to chaos. It then naturally leads to some form of authoritarianism to control the chaos. Having produced the sickness, humanism gives more of the same kind of medicine for the cure. With its mistaken concept of final reality, it has no intrinsic reason to be interested in the individual, the human being.[32]

Schaeffer also noted that most American leaders no longer consider themselves subject to God's laws. They often view themselves as answerable to no one. They do not acknowledge "inalienable rights" given to each individual by God. Instead, American leaders play God by distributing "rights" to individuals and by making their own arbitrary laws. Schaeffer quotes William Penn who said, "If we are not governed by God, then we will be ruled by tyrants."[33]

Schaeffer saw the 1973 legalization of abortion as a by-product of man playing God by legislating arbitrary laws and by the few forcing their will on the many.[34] But, according to

Schaeffer, this is just the beginning, for once human life has been devalued at one stage (i.e., the pre-birth stage), then no human life is safe. Abortion will lead to infanticide (the murdering of babies already born) and euthanasia (so called "mercy-killing").[35] Christianity teaches that human life is sacred because man was created in God's image, but now that modern man has rejected the Christian world view (the death of God), the death of man will follow (unless modern man repents) and man will be treated as non-man. Schaeffer documents the erosion of respect for human life in the statements of Nobel Prize winners Watson and Crick. These two scientists, after winning the Nobel Prize for cracking the genetic code, publicly recommended that we should terminate the lives of infants, three days old and younger, if they do not meet our expectations.[36]

In his response to behavioral scientist B. F. Skinner's book *Beyond Freedom and Dignity*, Schaeffer argued that Western culture's rejection of God, truth, and God's moral laws will lead to the death of man. Written in 1971, Skinner's book proposed a "utopian" society ruled by a small group of intellectual elitists who control the environment and genetic makeup of the masses. Schaeffer stated, "We are on the verge of the largest revolution the world has ever known—the control and shaping of men through the abuse of genetic knowledge, and chemical and psychological conditioning."[37] Schaeffer referred to Skinner's utopian proposals as "the death of man,"[38] and wrote concerning Skinner's low view of C. S. Lewis:

> Twice Skinner specifically attacked C. S. Lewis. Why? Because he is a Christian and writes in the tradition of the literatures of freedom and dignity. You will notice that he does not attack the evangelical church, probably because he doesn't think it's a threat to him. Unhappily, he is

largely right about this. Many of us are too sleepy to be a threat in the battle of tomorrow. But he understands that a man like C. S. Lewis, who writes literature which stirs men, is indeed a threat.[39]

Schaeffer understood not only the failure of secular humanism, but he also realized that Eastern pantheism offered no escape from the death of man. Only a return to the Christian world view could save the West from the death of man. He stated:

> Society can have no stability on this Eastern world-view or its present Western counterpart. It just does not work. And so one finds a gravitation toward some form of authoritarian government, an individual tyrant or group of tyrants who takes the reins of power and rule. And the freedoms, the sorts of freedoms we have enjoyed in the West, are lost. We are, then, brought back to our starting point. The inhumanities and the growing loss of freedoms in the West are the result of a world-view which has no place for "people." Modern humanistic materialism is an impersonal system. The East is no different. Both begin and end with impersonality.[40]

Schaeffer called upon evangelicals to sound the alarm, warning the church and society to repent, for the death of man is approaching:

> Learning from the mistakes of the past, let us raise a testimony that may still turn both the churches and society around—for the salvation of souls, the building of God's people, and at

least the slowing down of the slide toward a totally humanistic society and an authoritarian suppressive state.[41]

CONCLUDING REMARKS

Nietzsche wrote that Western culture's rejection of God would inevitably lead to the rejection of absolute truth and universal moral values. Allan Bloom confirmed that this has indeed been the case when he began his epic book *The Closing of the American Mind* with these words: "There is something a professor can be absolutely certain of: almost every student entering the university believes, or says he believes, that truth is relative."[42] Still, Nietzsche wrongly believed that this rejection of truth and morality would improve humanity by ushering in the "overman."

Lewis and Schaeffer agreed with Nietzsche's death of God, truth, and morality hypothesis, but, since they were Christians, they argued that this would not be an advancement for man. Instead, this would bring about the death of man. Though I believe that Lewis overstated his case by asserting that the death of man would create a "new species," I agree that, apart from Western culture's repentance, some type of death of man is inevitable. Man is presently being treated as non-man throughout the world (i.e., abortion, infanticide, euthanasia, religious persecution, genocide, violent crimes, etc.), and this trend will continue to increase apart from a return to the Christian world view.

As I see it, the death of man will involve spiritual, social, and psychological aspects. The death of man will be characterized by man being further alienated from God (the lost becoming harder to reach with the Gospel), from others (mankind becoming more and more depersonalized), and from himself (the light of man's moral conscience and his thirst for God will be dimmed). People, especially those in positions of authority, will treat other people as less than human. Man's love for man will grow cold.

To prevent, or at least slow down, the death of man, Christian thinkers must defend the reality of God, absolute truth, absolute moral values, as well as the dignity of man and the sanctity of human life. Still, we must do more than refute current ideologies; we must also proclaim to a complacent church and world where those ideas will take us in the twenty-first century if we refuse to repent. Like Lewis and Schaeffer, we must resist the temptation to pick dates for Christ's return or dogmatically declare that these are the last days, for we do not see the future with certainty— maybe Western culture will repent. Therefore, like Lewis, Schaeffer, and the Old Testament prophets, we must call our culture to repent. We must tell our generation that the nine-teenth century gave us the death of God, and the twentieth century gave us the death of truth and morality. Without widespread repentance, the twenty-first century will bring the death of man. Just as the removal of God from our schools has all but destroyed our public school system, the removal of God from the reigning ideas of Western culture will surely destroy our civilization. The death of God will ultimately lead to the death of man, if we do not turn back to the God of the Bible. Unless trends are reversed and the Christian world view is restored as the dominant perspective in Western culture, the twenty-first century will surpass the twentieth century in tyranny, violence, and ungodliness.

Though only God knows if we are actually in the final days, the words of our Savior warn us that someday the death of man will come:

> And this Gospel of the kingdom shall be preached in the whole world for a witness to all the nations, and then the end shall come. . . . for then there will be a great tribulation, such as has not occurred since the beginning of the world

until now, nor ever shall. And unless those days had been cut short, no life would have been saved; but for the sake of the elect those days shall be cut short (Matthew 24:14, 21-22).

ENDNOTES

[1] Friedrich Nietzsche, *The Portable Nietzsche*, ed. Walter Kaufman (New York: Penguin Books, 1968), 124, 447.

[2] Ibid., 143, 198.

[3] Norman L. Geisler and Paul D. Feinberg, *Introduction to Philosophy* (Grand Rapids: Baker Book House, 1980), 408.

[4] *The Portable Nietzsche*, 570.

[5] Geisler and Feinberg, 408.

[6] Ian P. McGreal, ed. *Great Thinkers of the Western World* (New York: HarperCollins Publishers, 1992), 409-410.

[7] *Portable Nietzsche*, 46-47.

[8] Frederick Copleston, A *History of Philosophy*, vol. VII (New York: Doubleday, 1963), 405-406.

[9] Stanley J. Grenz, *A Primer on Postmodernism* (Grand Rapids: William B. Eerdmans Publishing Co., 1996), 83.

[10] R. J. Rummel, *Death by Government* (New Brunswick: Transaction Publishers, 1997), 9. Rummel estimates that, in the twentieth century alone, between 170 and 360 million people have been killed by their own governments during times of peace. (This does not include the millions of unborn babies who were aborted in this century.)

[11] Peter Kreeft, *C. S. Lewis for the Third Millennium* (San Francisco: Ignatius Press, 1994), 107.

[12] C. S. Lewis, *The Abolition of Man* (New York: Collier Books, 1947), 23.

[13] Ibid., 16-17.

[14] Ibid., 28-29.

[15] Ibid., 34.

[16] Ibid., 77.

[17] Ibid., 39.

[18] Ibid., 62-63.

[19] Ibid., 69, 71.

[20] Ibid., 72.

[21] Ibid., 73-74.

[22] Ibid., 74.

[23] Ibid.

[24] Ibid., 78, 84.

[25] Ibid., 85.

[26] Ibid.

[27] Ibid., 85-86.

[28] Francis Schaeffer, *A Christian Manifesto* (Westchester: Crossway Books, 1981), 17-18.

[29] Francis Schaeffer, *The Complete Works of Francis A. Schaeffer*, vol. I (Westchester: Crossway Books, 1982), 8-11.

[30] Schaeffer, *A Christian Manifesto*, 48.

[31] Schaeffer, *Complete Works*, vol. V, 85-89.

[32] Schaeffer, *A Christian Manifesto*, 29-30.

[33] Ibid., 32-34.

[34] Ibid., 49.

[35] Schaeffer, *Complete Works*, vol. V, 317. see also vol. IV, 374.

[36] Ibid., vol. V, 319-320.

[37] Ibid., vol. I, 381.

[38] Ibid., 383.

[39] Ibid., 382-383.

[40] Ibid., vol. V, 381.

[41] Ibid., vol. IV, 364.

[42] Allan Bloom, *The Closing of the American Mind* (New York: Simon & Schuster, 1987), 25.

CHAPTER 12

THE NEW WORLD ORDER

By Rorri Wiesinger and Phil Fernandes

M any evangelical Christians (along with most Americans) ignore the ongoing formation of a one-world government, often referred to as the "New World Order." They do not want to be accused of espousing some type of "conspiracy theory." However, global government *is* becoming a reality and Christians must take a stand against it. It is our Christian duty to expose evil and oppose the spirit of the age.

Former President George H. W. Bush often referred to "The New World Order" in his speeches during the Persian Gulf War. Bush made it clear that the UN would head the New World Order and that international law would and should be enforced by the UN.

Many Americans, including numerous political leaders, believe that global government is the best way to achieve and sustain world peace. Many New Agers, secular humanists, American communists, liberal politicians, and neo-conservative politicians agree that the best (or only) way to guarantee global peace and prosperity is through a one-world socialist economy, international laws, and an all-powerful UN peace-keeping force. Besides the concern for global peace, other factors such as poverty, environmental issues, the ecumenical movement (the attempt to unite all the religions of the world), and the fear of overpopulation make the idea of one-world government an appealing prospect to many.

However, Bible-believing Christians must oppose the movement towards a one-world government. Because mankind is fallen, no human or group of humans should be given absolute control over the lives of billions. Only Jesus, as the Prince of Peace (Isaiah 9:6), has the right to reign over the entire earth. We should trust in Jesus alone for peace, not the UN and the wisdom of man (Psalm 118:8-9). A one-world government (without Jesus as its King) may produce the end-time kingdom of the Antichrist and the mark of the beast (Revelation 13). It will never produce peace and justice (Daniel 9:26; 1 Thessalonians 5:3). God-ordained human government has a limited role (to serve its citizens by protecting their God-given human rights) and limited power. Unlimited global government will not serve mankind; it will enslave mankind.

THE TWENTIETH CENTURY

An overview of the twentieth century will show the conscious merging of the U.S. government with various supranational organizations and institutions. Through multiple and international agreements and treaties, the U.S. and other nations have set upon a course leading to international government. Evidence for this has been sufficiently documented through various sources.[1]

In 1913, the Federal Reserve System was created. The Federal Reserve is a central bank with an exclusive monopoly to issue fiat currency (i.e., currency not backed by gold or silver). The Fed is run by private investment bankers who control the U.S. economy through inflation and deflation of its currency. Congress created the Federal Reserve with no constitutional authorization. Its bankers are not accountable to Congress or to the people, and they cannot be removed by the people through an election process. Hence, they have dictatorial authority to create boom and bust cycles, which they fully exploit in order to advance their socialist and globalist agendas.

The economic crash of 1929 provides a clear example of the Federal Reserve's nefarious ability to manipulate and destroy an economy. In a calculated move, the Fed reduced the quantity of currency causing a deflationary effect that sank the Stock Market and initiated the Great Depression of the 1930's. With the economic depression in high gear, the Federal Reserve's brain trust had the necessary pretext for the introduction of President Franklin Roosevelt's economic "reforms" known as the New Deal. Roosevelt's socialist New Deal was patterned after the statist policies of Italy's fascist dictator, Benito Mussolini.

A close political ally of Franklin Roosevelt and one of America's most notorious political insiders, Edward M. House had played a pivotal role with the planning and creation of the graduated federal income tax, the League of Nations, and the Council on Foreign Relations.

As President Woodrow Wilson's chief advisor, House was able to exert his tremendous political influence into Wilson's domestic and foreign policies. It cannot be overstated that House was both an ardent internationalist and committed Marxist. In his thinly veiled 1912 novel *Philip Dru: Administrator*, House wrote that he desired "socialism as dreamed of by Karl Marx."

House, working with British and American internationalists, helped to found the Council on Foreign Relations in

1921. This was due to the fact that America had refused to join the League of Nations following World War I. If another attempt to bring the United States into an international body was to succeed, the thinking of American leaders had to change. Therefore, the Council on Foreign Relations was formed to persuade key American leaders that the answer to the world's greatest challenges was the establishment of a socialist world government. Hence, a gradual erosion of the sovereignty of the United States government had to occur.

Today, the CFR has over 3,000 members; the vast majority of which occupy top positions in finance, industry, business, government, defense, education, and the media. The CFR has often been called the "American establishment" since the State department has been controlled by CFR members for decades. The CFR has maintained control of the State Department regardless of whether the President is a Democrat or Republican. Since Eisenhower, every U.S. president, except Reagan and George W. Bush, has been a member of the Council on Foreign Relations. Even in the Ronald Reagan and George W. Bush administrations, the President's cabinet was filled with key CFR members. Today, it is almost impossible to be a national leader in either of the major political parties without CFR membership. Prominent CFR members include George H. W. Bush, Henry Kissinger, Zbigniew Brzezinski, Alan Greenspan, David Rockefeller, Bill Clinton, and Newt Gingrich.

The CFR publishes a journal called *Foreign Affairs* dealing with U.S. foreign policy. If one closely reads these journals, one will see that the issue of global government is not open to debate. The only questions open for discussion are the rate of increase concerning the movement toward world government and the ways and methods through which it will be achieved. Questions that challenge the pro-globalist orthodoxy, however, are not open for discussion.

In 1943 CFR members directed the Roosevelt State Department to draft the proposal for the founding of the United Nations. The United Nations was a second attempt at the failed League of Nations. After the end of World War II, representatives from 50 nations, including the United States, signed the United Nations Organization charter in San Francisco on June 26, 1945. This marked the birth of the UN.

U.S. State Department official Alger Hiss, a CFR member, was the first UN Secretary General. It later became known that Hiss was an American Communist Party member and a soviet agent. The empowerment of the UN was one of the chief goals of the communist party in America.

Every major war that America has been involved in since World War II has been directed by or under UN subsidiary alliances such as NATO or SEATO (i.e., Korea, Vietnam, Panama, Iraq, Somalia, Haiti, Bosnia, Kosovo, etc.). It should also be noted that the UN's top military official is the UN Secretary General of Political Affairs. This post has been filled by a Soviet Russian since the UN's founding.

Many Americans believe that the UN offers no threat to U.S. sovereignty since it has no "teeth" (i.e., no military power). However, this perspective is easily refuted once we realize that the U.S. military (the most powerful military on earth) seems to work exclusively for UN goals, and ultimately under UN command. According to the U.S. Constitution, only the U.S. Congress has the power to declare war. The last constitutional war the U.S. was involved in was World War II. All wars or military "conflicts" in which America has been involved since World War II have been to serve the interests of the UN. It appears that the UN has "teeth" (i.e., the United States military).

Today, there exist many UN-based subsidiary and regional organizations such as: the International Monetary Fund (IMF), the European Union (EU), the World Bank (WB), the International Criminal Court (ICC), the North

Atlantic Treaty Organization (NATO), the World Trade Organization (WTO), the UN Education, Scientific, and Cultural Organization (UNESCO), the United Religions Organization (URO), the World Court (WC), and the World Health Organization (WHO). These organizations are extremely influential in the affairs of the nations of the world. The gradual usurpations of national sovereignty by UN institutions show the UN to be a global government in the embryo stage.

Official policies of the United States government since the 1960's reveal that U.S. strategy is threefold: 1) gradually disarm and weaken the US military, 2) progressively strengthen UN military capabilities, and 3) the peaceful merger of the United States with Russia. This threefold strategy is spelled out in several executive and congressional policies.

Memorandum No. 7: A World Effectively Controlled by the UN was a study funded by the U.S. State Department during the Kennedy administration and completed in February, 1961. It showed how U.S. military disarmament could be achieved in order to further the cause of global governance.

U.S. executive policy *Freedom From War: The US Program for General and Complete Disarmament in a Peaceful World* (Department of State Publication 7277, September, 1961) presents a three-stage program for the gradual transfer of U.S. armaments to UN control.

U.S. Congressional Policy *US Public Law 87-297—the Arms Control and Disarmament Act* —was signed into law by President Kennedy on September 26, 1961. This law created the U.S. Arms Control and Disarmament Agency that was designed to advance efforts toward complete disarmament of the world's nations, while excluding the UN, thus attempting to give the UN a monopoly on military power. *Blueprint for the Peace Race: Outline of Basic Provisions of a Treaty on General and Complete Disarmament in a Peaceful World* (U.S. Arms Control and Disarmament Agency Publication No. 4, April 1962) is a U.S. State Department document that superseded the earlier *Freedom From War* document. *Blueprint for the Peace Race* remains official U.S. policy and continues the same three-stage U.S. disarmament program of the *Freedom from War* document while progressively strengthening UN military capabilities.

Project Phoenix: Study Phoenix Paper (June, 1963) is a U.S. State Department funded study produced by the Institute of Defense Analyses for the U.S. Arms Control and Disarmament Agency which openly advocates U.S. and Soviet unification. On June 17, 1992, President George H. W. Bush and Russian President Boris Yeltsin fulfilled much of the spirit of *Project Phoenix* by signing the official convergence document entitled *Charter for American/ Russian Partnership and Friendship.*

In 1993 and 1994, President Clinton issued Presidential Decision Directives that expanded the UN's peace-keeping missions around the world and permitted U.S. military forces to be placed under foreign command in UN operations on a case by case basis (PDD-13 and PDD-25).

KEY GLOBALIST ORGANIZATIONS

Besides the CFR and UN, other key globalist organizations include the Bilderberger Group, the Club of Rome, the Trilateral Commission, and the European Union. The Bilderberger Group was launched by Prince Bernhard of Holland and David Rockefeller in 1954 at the Bilderberger Hotel in Oosterbeek, Holland. This elite group consists of prominent internationalists who meet annually to discuss their globalist agendas for the upcoming year and beyond. The media is strictly prohibited from covering these secret meetings. Although key leaders of the media are occasionally invited to attend a Bilderberger meeting, they do not divulge the details of the meeting.

The European Union can trace its roots back to 1951 when the European Coal and Steel Community (ECSC) was formed. From the ECSC, the gradual political merger of the European nations began to progress steadily. In 1957, the Treaty of Rome established the European Economic Community (EEC), also known as the Common Market, and the European Atomic Community (EURATOM). In 1967, the ECSC, the EEC, and EURATOM merged to form the European Community (EC). In a major push to establish monetary and political union, the Maastricht Treaty of 1991 was signed by EC member nations. The Maastricht treaties went into effect in 1993, and the European Union (EU) was born.

In 1968, the Club of Rome was founded by New Ager Aurelio Peccei (a disciple of the late New Age thinker Pierre Teilhard de Chardin) for the purpose of unifying the world under a single authority. In a work entitled *Mankind at the Turning Point*, Mihajlo Mesarovic and Eduard Pestel, two Club of Rome Members, stated that the Club of Rome divided the world into 10 regions, and that, to ensure the survival of the human race, mankind must no longer cooperate on the national level, but on the global level. (Some Bible prophecy experts believe these 10 regions may be the "10 kingdoms" of the end-time world government headed by the antichrist and spoken about in Revelation 13:1; 17:12-14; and Daniel 2:40-42; 7:23-24.)

Inspired by the world government concepts outlined in Columbia University professor Zbigniew Brzezinski's book *Between Two Ages*, David Rockefeller founded the Trilateral Commission in 1973. Zbigniew Brzezinski, who later became the National Security Advisor for President Carter, drew up the Commission's charter and became its first director. The purpose of the Trilateral Commission is to expedite the formation of a world government by encouraging economic interdependence between the world's three economic superpowers (the United States, Western Europe, and Japan).

KEY GLOBALIST LEADERS

Other key globalists include Mikhail Gorbachev, former UN Secretary General Boutros Boutros-Gahli, Maurice Strong (Secretary General of the Earth Summit), former UN Assistant Secretary General Robert Muller, and the late Georgetown University Professor Caroll Quigley. Gorbachev heads the Green Cross organization through which he promotes radical environmentalism and worship of the earth. In a 1992 speech at Westminster College in Missouri, Gorbachev expressed "the need for some kind of global government." Gorbachev also hosts some of the world's leading globalists at his State of the World Forums.

Boutros Boutros-Gahli wrote a book entitled *An Agenda for Peace* in which he called for an end to national sovereignty. Boutros-Gahli sees the UN as man's only hope for global peace.

Maurice Strong is a close friend of David Rockefeller and the driving force behind the UN environmental policy. Strong is a fervent New Ager who headed the Earth Summit, also known as the United Nations Conference on Environment and Development. Strong worked with Gorbachev in producing and promoting the Earth Charter, supposedly a bill of rights for the people of the earth. The Earth Charter calls for a new morality with radical environmentalism and worship of the earth at its foundation.

Though Robert Muller officially retired in 1986, he continues to diligently work for the cause of world government. Muller is very active in the area of education and is the author of *The World Core Curriculum*, a document which promotes globalism and New Age beliefs. This document earned Muller the title "the Father of Global Education." The

UN has pushed for The *World Core Curriculum* to be accepted as the foundation for education throughout the world. In fact, *Goals 2000* in America was inspired by *The World Core Curriculum*. Muller's thought was influenced by New Agers Teilhard de Chardin and Alice Bailey of the Theosophical Society. Muller's ideas were instrumental in bringing the United Religions Initiative (the UN's current attempt to unite all the religions of the world) into existence.

The late Georgetown Professor, Caroll Quigley, himself a globalist, wrote a massive book entitled *Tragedy and Hope: A History of Our Time*. Written in 1966, this book gives the details of the globalist agenda from the perspective of an insider. Quigley's most famous student was William Jefferson Clinton.

LEADING OPPONENTS OF THE NEW WORLD ORDER

There have been a few American leaders with the courage to speak out against the above anti-American organizations. In the 1950's Congressman Carroll Reece headed the Reece Committee, which investigated major tax-exempt foundations such as the Rockefeller, Carnegie, and Ford Foundations. The Reece Committee discovered that these foundations donated large sums of money to control the social sciences, public education, and international affairs. The Committee found that these foundations financed the CFR and other globalist organizations.

In the 1970's, Senator Barry Goldwater publicly spoke out against the New World Order on numerous occasions. He had the courage to identify key globalist organizations and denounce their hideous agendas.

In 1981, Congressman Larry McDonald called for a congressional investigation into the CFR and the Trilateral Commission. Unfortunately, his life and investigation were tragically cut short in 1983 when he was killed (along with

268 other passengers) when the Korean Air Lines flight 007 was shot down by Soviet air-to-air missiles. The American media reported the incident as an unfortunate "accident."

In 1987, Senator Jesse Helms publicly spoke out against the "Eastern Establishment," the Council on Foreign Relations, the Trilateral Commission, the Bilderberger Group, and the Federal Reserve System. He stated that the establishment's view was once called "one-world," but that it is now known as "globalism." In recent years, Senator Helms has not been as outspoken against the New World Order as he was in the 1980's.

In the 1980's and 1990's, presidential candidate Pat Buchanan railed against the New World Order in his campaign speeches. This may be one of the primary reasons for his failure to win the presidency. The American media portrayed Buchanan as a bigot, a common tactic utilized by the press against true conservative candidates.

Currently, Congressman Ron Paul is the leading spokesman against the globalist agenda. On a regular basis, he calls upon his fellow congressmen to vote for the United States' removal from the United Nations, but only a small percentage of our congressmen support Congressman Paul on this account.

It is our Christian duty to pray for leaders like Congressman Paul as they fight the forces of evil behind enemy lines. But we must do more than pray. God is calling us to speak out against the New World Order just as He called Christians to speak out against the holocaust, slavery, and abortion. By remaining silent, we help tomorrow's tyrants build the New World Order and enslave the masses.

ENDNOTES

[1] Tal Brooke, *One World* (Berkeley: End Run Publishing, 2000). William F. Jasper, *Global Tyranny: Step By Step* (Appleton: Western Islands, 1992). William Norman Grigg, *Freedom on the Altar* (Appleton: American Opinion

Publishing, Inc., 1995). John F. McManus, *Changing Commands* (Appleton: The John Birch Society, 1995). James Perloff, *The Shadows of Power* (Appleton: Western Islands, 1988). Gary H. Kah, *En Route to Global Occupation* (Lafayette: Huntington House, 1992). Gary H. Kah, *The New World Religion* (Noblesville, Indiana: Hope International, 1998). Dean Isaacson, *Under the Tower of Babel* (Monroe, Washington: Cominus Books, 1995). Michael S. Coffman, *Saviors of the Earth?* (Chicago: Northfield Publishing, 1994). John F. McManus, *Financial Terrorism* (Appleton: John Birch Society, 1993). John F. McManus, *The Insiders* (Appleton: John Birch Society, 1996).

CHAPTER 13

THE RETURN TO BABEL: GOD'S VIEW OF THE UNITED NATIONS

by Phil Fernandes

The United Nations is leading the way, pulling the separate countries of the world into a one-world government. In the eyes of many we are entering a new age of global peace. No longer will nations war with each other. Mankind has brought peace to the world.

Before jumping on the "peace at any price" bandwagon, Christians should turn to God's Word to find His view of world government. A person need only read the eleventh chapter of Genesis to find God's view of a one-world government. In this chapter, the peoples of the earth have settled together in one area of the earth. This is despite God's command that they fill the earth (Genesis 1:28). God saw that mankind spoke one common language and that they had one common purpose (Genesis 11:1-6). Contrary to what many modern men and women would expect, God was not pleased. God did not like the idea of mankind united into one government while they were still in rebellion against Him. God knew that one language and a one-world government would increase technology greatly (Genesis 11:6); still, He recognized that this would only accelerate man's demise.

God decided to scatter mankind and confuse their language (Genesis 11:7-9). This forced men to live in separate nations (Genesis 10:25). Apparently, God was not pleased with a one-world government.

God's Word tells us that there will be wars until the end (Daniel 9:26; Matthew 24:6-7). Mankind will not be able to bring global peace to earth. Only when Jesus, the Prince of Peace, returns will man have the peace he has desired (Isaiah 9:6-7; 2:1-4). A one-world government will only increase the level of violence and destruction on this planet. For the leader of the future one-world government will be none other than the antichrist, a demon-possessed end-time ruler who will rule the world and oppress the masses (Revelation 13:1-18).

God instituted human government for two reasons. First, because man was created in God's image. Therefore, human life is sacred and needs to be protected (Genesis 9:6). Second, humans are sinful (due to the fall of man in the garden); therefore, evil needs to be restrained (Romans 13:1-4). Hence, God instituted human government to protect human life and to restrain evil.

The Word of God also indicates why human government must be limited. The Bible teaches that humans are sinful (Romans 3:10, 23). Since human governments are run by humans, and all humans are sinful, then the powers of those who rule must be limited. This is a biblical principle that our founding fathers clearly understood. They enacted several measures to insure the limiting of the rulers' power. First, they recognized God as above the government by acknowledging the unalienable rights of men and women. Second, they believed that nations should be separate (they were opposed to surrendering United States' sovereignty). Third, they set up a system of checks and balances and a separation of powers to limit the power of human leaders. They established a separation of powers between federal, state, and local governments. They instituted a separation of powers between the three branches of government (executive, judicial, and legislative). And, fourth, our founding fathers limited the power of human government by recognizing the people's right to worship, vote, protest, and bear arms.

God is opposed to a one-world government ruled by men. Our founding fathers were right to limit the power of government. Only when Jesus returns can mankind have true and lasting peace. Only when Jesus returns shall we have a God-ordained one-world government (Revelation 19:11-16; 20:1-6), for, only then will the Kingdom of God have come to earth (Revelation 11:15).

CHAPTER 14

REFUTING MORAL RELATIVISM

by Phil Fernandes

E thics is the branch of philosophy that deals with issues of morality, that which is right and wrong.[1] The Christian ethical perspective holds to absolute moral values, laws that are universally binding. Often, non-Christian views hold to moral relativism. Moral relativists reject the idea that there are universal rights and wrongs.[2] What is right for one person is not necessarily right for another person, and vice versa. Each person decides what is right for himself. Many atheists and pantheists are moral relativists.[3]

AN EXAMINATION OF MORAL RELATIVISM

Friedrich Nietzsche (1844-1900) was a German philosopher who believed that the advances of human knowledge had proven that belief in God was a mere superstition. Nietzsche therefore reasoned that since "God is dead," all traditional values have died with Him. Nietzsche was angered with his atheistic colleagues who were unwilling to dismiss traditional moral absolutes which had no justification without God's existence.[4]

Nietzsche preached that a group of "supermen" must arise with the courage to create their own values through their "will to power." Nietzsche rejected the "soft" values of Christianity (brotherly love, turning the other cheek, charity, compassion, etc.); he felt they hindered man's creativity and potential. He recommended that the supermen create their own "hard" values that would allow man to realize his creative potential.[5] Nietzsche was very consistent with his atheism. He realized that without God, there are no universal moral values. Man is free to create his own values. It is interesting to note that the Nazis often referred to Nietzsche's writings for the supposed intellectual justification for their acts of cruelty.[6]

Many other atheists agree with Nietzsche concerning moral relativism. British philosopher Bertrand Russell (1872-1970) once wrote, "Outside human desires there is no moral standard."[7] A. J. Ayer believed that moral commands did not result from any objective standard above man. Instead, Ayer stated that moral commands merely express one's subjective feelings. When one says that murder is wrong, one is merely saying that he feels that murder is wrong.[8] Jean-Paul Sartre, a French existentialist, believed that there is no objective meaning to life. Therefore, according to Sartre, man must create his own values.[9]

There are many different ways that moral relativists attempt to determine what action should be taken. Hedonism is probably the most extreme. It declares that whatever brings the most pleasure is right. In other words, if it feels good, do it.[10] If this position is true, then there is no basis from which to judge the actions of Adolph Hitler as being evil.[11]

Utilitarianism teaches that man should attempt to bring about the greatest good for the greatest number of people.[12] However, utilitarianism is problematic. First, "good" is a meaningless term if moral relativism is true, for then there would be no such thing as good or evil. Second, to say that man "should" do something is to introduce a universal moral command. However, there is no room for universal moral commands in moral relativism.[13]

Joseph Fletcher founded "situation ethics." Situation ethics is the view that ethics are relative to the situation. Fletcher claimed that he was not a moral relativist. He believed that there was only one moral absolute: love. Still, his concept of love was so void of meaning that his view of ethics, for all practical purposes, is synonymous with moral relativism.[14]

Christian philosopher Norman Geisler notes that the situation never determines what is right. It is God who determines what is right. Still, the situation may aid the Christian in finding which of God's laws should be applied.[15] For when two of God's commands come in conflict due to a situation so that a person cannot obey both, God requires that the person obey the greater command. God then exempts the person from obeying the lesser command. An example of this is the fact that God compliments Rahab the Harlot for lying in order to save two innocent lives (Joshua 2; Hebrews 11:31; James 2:25).[16]

REFUTING MORAL RELATIVISM

Moral relativists deny the absolute moral law. Still, they, like all people, recognize the evil actions of others when they are wronged. When they are wronged, they appeal to an objective and universal law that stands above man. Moral relativists deny the absolute moral law in the lecture hall, but they live by it in their everyday lives.[17] Moral relativists reserve the right for themselves to call the actions of Hitler wrong,[18] but, if there is no such thing as right and wrong (as the moral relativists say), they cannot really call any action wrong.

The moral law does not ultimately come from within each individual, for then no one could call the actions of another, such as Hitler, evil.[19] The moral law does not ultimately come from each society, for then one society could not call the actions of another society (such as Nazi Germany) wrong.[20] Finally, the moral law does not ultimately come from world consensus,[21] for world consensus is often wrong. World consensus once thought the world was flat and that slavery was morally permissible.

Appealing to world or societal consensus as the ultimate source of the moral law is actually just an extension of the view that the individual is the ultimate source. The difference is only quantitative (the number of people increases). However, for there to be a moral law above all men (in order to judge all men), this moral law must be qualitatively above all men. If there is an absolute moral law qualitatively above all men, all societies, and the world consensus, then there must be an absolute moral law Giver that stands qualitatively above all men, all societies, and world consensus.

The absolute moral law is eternal and unchanging, for we use it to condemn the actions of past generations. Since the moral law is eternal and unchanging, the moral law Giver must also be eternal and unchanging. The moral law is not descriptive of what is; it is prescriptive of what should be.[22] Prescriptive laws need a Prescriber.

Since the absolute moral law leads directly to the existence of the theistic God (the absolute moral law Giver), many atheists and pantheists may feel compelled to reject it's existence. On the other hand, people who wish to live promiscuous lives often choose to reject God's existence. The apostle John appears to be talking about these people:

> And this is the judgment, that the light is come
> into the world, and men loved the darkness rather
> than the light; for their deeds were evil. For
> everyone who does evil hates the light, and does
> not come to the light, lest his deeds should be
> exposed (John 3:19-20).

ENDNOTES

[1] Geisler and Feinberg, *Introduction to Philosophy* (Grand Rapids: Baker Book House, 1980), 24-26.

[2] Moreland, *Scaling the Secular City* (Grand Rapids: Baker Book House, 1987), 240.

[3] Geisler and Watkins, *Worlds Apart* (Grand Rapids: Baker Book House, 1989), 59, 99-100.

[4] Friedrich Nietzsche, *The Portable Nietzsche*, trans. Walter Kaufman (New York: Penguin Books, 1982), 95-96, 143, 228.

[5] Ibid., 124-125, 139, 191, 197-198.

[6] Frederick Copleston, *A History of Philosophy* (New York: Image Books, 1963), vol. 7, 403.

[7] Bertrand Russell, *Why I Am Not A Christian* (New York: Touchstone Books, 1957), 62.

[8] Norman L. Geisler, Christian Ethics (Grand Rapids: Baker Book House, 1989), 32.

[9] Geisler and Feinberg, 406.

[10] Ibid., 400-401.

[11] Geisler, *Christian Ethics*, 36-37.

[12] Ibid., 63.

[13] Ibid., 73-75.

[14] Ibid., 43-61.

[15] Geisler and Feinberg, 411.

[16] Ibid., 424-427.

[17] Hodge, *Systematic Theology* (Grand Rapids: Eerdmans Publishing, 1989), vol. 1, 210.

[18] Hick, *The Existence of God* (New York: MacMillan Company, 1964), 183-186.

[19] Moreland, 246-247.

[20] Ibid., 243-244.

[21] Geisler and Feinberg, 355.

[22] C. S. Lewis, *Mere Christianity* (New York: Collier Books, 1952), 27-28.

CHAPTER 15

THE NEW TOLERANCE

by Phil Fernandes

GOD'S MORAL ABSOLUTES

As the *Declaration of Independence* made clear, the American society and government were founded upon the biblical view of morality. In both the Bible and the conscience of each person, God had revealed His moral laws that were true for all people at all times in all places. For the first 100 years of American independence this acceptance of God's moral absolutes reigned supreme as the dominant view of American society.

NO MORAL ABSOLUTES (MORAL RELATIVISM)

In 1859 Charles Darwin published his Origin of Species, in which he proposed a scientific model of the universe which explained away the need for God as Creator or Sustainer of the universe. As Darwin's views became popular in America, respect for God's absolute moral laws began to decline.

Eventually, the leading view in the American media and colleges became moral relativism—the rejection of moral absolutes—the belief that what is right for one person may not be right for another person, and vice versa. John Dewey, known as "the father of modern education," was a moral relativist, and he spread his views to his pupils—the future teachers in the American public school system.

Suddenly, all behavior was viewed as equally good. Moral value judgments were unacceptable. God's moral laws had been rejected by the opinion molders of the American culture.

NEW MORAL ABSOLUTES

As moral relativism became more widespread, it was considered "wrong" to condemn the actions or lifestyle of another person as "wrong" (due to the belief that there is no such thing as "wrong"). As contradictory as this view is, it became more popular in American culture as time progressed. In today's world, it is morally right to be a moral relativist, but it is morally wrong to acknowledge traditional moral values. The Bible speaks of a time when God's chosen nation (Israel/Judah) had rejected His moral laws and substituted these laws with a new morality. God warned Judah, "Woe to those who call evil good, and good evil" (Isaiah 5:20). We Americans are living in such a climate today. If God judged Judah for abandoning His moral laws, He will also judge us if we continue to do the same.

William Watkins has authored a book entitled *The New Absolutes* in which he argues that America has moved beyond the stage of moral relativism (no absolutes) to the stage of new absolutes (where evil is good and good is evil).[1] Watkins shows that the new absolutes declare traditional religion (i.e., Christianity, Judaism, etc.) to be harmful and that it should be banned from public life, human life is no longer sacred, and sexual promiscuity and homosexuality are morally healthy lifestyles.[2] Anyone who disagrees with the new morality is viewed as intolerant and may even be guilty of a "hate crime."

THE TRADITIONAL VIEW OF TOLERANCE

The traditional view of tolerance encouraged the freedom of religious expression and the freedom of speech.[3] The Christian had the right to believe and proclaim that anyone who rejects Jesus as Savior will spend eternity in torment. The Muslim had the right to preach that only good Muslims will go to heaven. The traditional view of tolerance promoted dialogue between people who disagreed on religious, political, or moral issues. It upheld a person's right to disagree with others without fear of imprisonment or censorship; it respected the views of others even when they disagreed with your own beliefs.

THE NEW TOLERANCE

The traditional view of tolerance has been replaced by a new definition of tolerance. Josh McDowell and Bob Hostetler explain the difference between the traditional view and the new view:

> In contrast to traditional tolerance, which asserts that everyone has an equal right to believe or say what he thinks is right, the new tolerance—the way our children are being taught to believe—says that what every individual believes or says is equally right, equally valid. So not only does everyone have an equal right to his beliefs, but all beliefs are equal. All values are equal. All lifestyles are equal. All truth claims are equal.[4]

In the name of tolerance, traditional beliefs are no longer tolerated. The goal of the new tolerance is not to get people to respect and tolerate the lifestyles and beliefs of all people. Instead, the goal of the new tolerance is to attempt to force everyone to "approve of and participate in" the attitudes and activities of the new morality.[5] This new "tolerance" is rapidly becoming a religion of tolerance; however, it has the potential to be the most intolerant religion in the history of mankind. Those who choose to reject the new tolerance (also known as "the new morality" or "political correctness") are often "branded as narrow-minded bigots, fanatics, extremists, and hatemongers and subjected to public humiliation and indoctrination."[6]

One of the members of my church works for a large nationally known store chain. When he received his "diversity training," he was informed that he would not be allowed to greet customers by saying "God bless you" because this would be offensive to many people and infringe upon their rights. He was told he could read his Bible during his break time so long as he did not share his beliefs with other workers or customers. No such restrictions were placed upon his homosexual co-workers. This is a clear example of the new tolerance. Whereas the traditional view of tolerance promoted freedom of religion and freedom of speech, the new tolerance only allows for those freedoms if you are an adherent of the new tolerance. The new tolerance proclaims, "I am all for your freedoms of speech and religion so long as your share my views and my religion. Any other views are unacceptable and cannot be tolerated." The new tolerance is intolerant with a vengeance.

Unfortunately, this new tolerance is not limited to American soil. The United Nations, which may someday rule the world, also adheres to the new tolerance. The United Nations *Declaration of Principles on Tolerance* states that "Tolerance . . . involves the rejection of dogmaticism and absolutism."[7] Obviously, this is a self-contradictory statement, for the rejection of dogmaticism is itself a dogma, and the rejection of absolutism is itself an absolute. In the name of the new tolerance, traditional Americans, in some cases, have been denied "schooling, scholarships, and employment."[8] In 1995, a US District judge from Texas "ruled that any student mentioning the name of Jesus in a graduation prayer would be sentenced to a six-month jail term."[9] It seems that anyone who holds to absolute standards (God's moral absolutes) will eventually lose their freedom of speech and be silenced so that politically-correct "progress" may continue.[10]

THE STAGES OF THE DECAY OF A CIVILIZATION

In Romans 1:18-32, the Apostle Paul spells out what I call "the stages of the decay of a civilization." The first stage is *the rejection of the God of creation* (vs 18-22). Even though the invisible God has clearly revealed His existence to man through His visible creation, many people (and civilizations) continue to reject Him. The second stage is *idolatry*, the worship of false gods. The worship of the creation replaces the worship of the Creator God (vs 23-25). The third stage is *widespread sexual immorality and wickedness* (vs 26-31). Paul emphasizes the sinful homosexual lifestyle as characteristic of this stage. But the fourth and final stage of decay of a civilization is *the active acceptance and promotion of evil* (vs 32). Today, this is called "political correctness," "the new morality," or "the new tolerance." America, as well as all of Western Civilization, is at this final stage of decay. God's judgment is near.

In short, the new tolerance is no tolerance at all. If it continues to become more widespread, it will lead to the persecution of traditional Christians and Jews, but it will also bring God's judgment. Therefore, America must heed God's warning, "Woe to those who call evil good, and good evil" (Isaiah 5:20).

ENDNOTES

[1] William D. Watkins, *The New Absolutes* (Minneapolis: Bethany House Publishers, 1996).

[2] Ibid., 45, 65, 89, 99, 113, 131, 207.

[3] Josh McDowell and Bob Hostetler, *The New Tolerance* (Wheaton: Tyndale House Publishers, 1998), 18.

[4] Ibid., 19-20.

[5] Ibid., 31.

[6] Ibid., 32.

[7] Ibid., 43.

[8] Ibid., 32.

[9] Ibid., 53.

[10] Ibid., 56.

CHAPTER 16

A NATION UNDER GOD'S JUDGMENT

by Phil Fernandes

═══════════════════════════

Though America was originally founded upon biblical principles, our nation has turned its back on the God who has blessed us so abundantly. I am convinced that, if we do not repent, God will judge this nation.

There are several reasons why I believe that America is under God's judgment. First, we live in a country that kills many of its own unborn children before they see the light of day. In fact, it is now legal in America to kill babies who are partially born. A doctor can legally pull a baby's body, except for the head, outside of the mother's womb, puncture the baby's skull, and insert a suction device to suck out the baby's brains. The Bible declares that the Lord hates "hands that shed innocent blood" (Proverbs 6:16-17).

Second, sexual immorality is becoming more and more widespread in this country. God gave mankind the gift of sex to be enjoyed between a husband and his wife (Matthew 19:3-6). Today, premarital sex, adultery, sexual promiscuity, and homosexuality are not only widely practiced, but are often promoted through the media. God will not allow these practices to go unpunished (Leviticus 18:19-25). Just as He punished Sodom and Gomorrah for sexual immorality, so too God will judge America if we do not repent (Genesis 19:1-26). If America wants to avoid judgment, our "politically correct" mantras promoting immoral lifestyles must be stifled by the proclamation of God's truth to a nation gone astray.

Third, America is becoming more and more violent. This is the logical outcome of a society that teaches its youth that there is no such thing as right and wrong (moral relativism). God will not tolerate violent crimes such as murder and rape (Genesis 6:11-13). Ironically, our leaders allow criminals to walk the streets while, in most major cities, prohibiting law-abiding citizens from carrying firearms to protect themselves. This only increases the potential for violence.

Fourth, the American government has become more and more intolerant of the Christian Faith and the spreading of the Gospel. We have attempted to remove God from our public schools, secular universities, and the political arena. We no longer acknowledge and thank the God who has blessed us so abundantly.

Fifth, American foreign policy appears to be turning against the nation of Israel (God's chosen nation) and siding with her enemies. Though America is clearly the best friend that Israel has among the nations, our officials often try to dictate policy to Israel concerning their sworn enemies. Our leaders often discourage Israel from retaliating for acts of terrorism perpetrated against her and pressure the Israeli government to surrender portions of her land to her Arab enemies (supposedly to promote "peace" in the region). God promised Abraham that He would bless those who bless his descendants (the nation of Israel) and curse those who curse his descendants (Genesis 12:1-3). History has proven this true time and time again. Nations or empires that have come against Israel have been devastated. If America chooses to oppose Israel, the fate of our nation will be no different from that of Babylon, Rome, the Philistines, Nazi Germany, and the Soviet Union (some of Israel's past enemies). The fact that we have backed Israel in the past may be the primary reason why God has postponed our judgment.

Other reasons why God has chosen to spare us from the judgment we deserve may be the fact that America has led the world concerning foreign missions (the spreading of the Gospel worldwide) and the charitable deeds our people do for less fortunate people around the globe. Still, for the reasons listed above, if America does not repent, judgment is coming.

In short, America is not beyond God's judgment. We have forsaken the God of the Bible, and, if we do not repent, judgment will come. The warning proclaimed by Isaiah the prophet applies to America today: "Woe to those who call evil good and good evil" (Isaiah 5:20). Our only hope is for Americans throughout this land to confess their sins and call out to the Lord Jesus for forgiveness (2 Chronicles 7:14). We must pray for our nation, forsake our wicked ways, and turn to Jesus for salvation. Without true revival, America will fall.

CHAPTER 17

DEFENDING THE HELPLESS

by Phil Fernandes

A partial-birth abortion is a procedure whereby the fetus is partially removed, legs first, from its mother's womb and the brain of the fetus is drained through the use of a suction tube. Recently, Congress proposed a bill to ban this cruel practice. However, President Clinton vetoed the bill, and Congress was unable to override the his veto.

The partial-birth abortion reveals the true colors of the pro-abortion movement (also known as the "pro-choice movement" by its friends in the secular media). The intellectual elite heading the pro-abortion movement has recognized for years that the unborn child is a human being and that human life begins at conception. Only on the popular level is it argued that the unborn child is not a human being.

Watson and Crick, the scientists who won the Nobel Prize for cracking the genetic code, have publicly stated that since we have arbitrarily declared that human life does not start until birth, we have begun to play God. But, Watson and Crick are not opposed to man playing God. In fact, they like the idea. They suggest we add a trial period and not declare a baby alive until after the third day following birth. In this way, the parents and doctors could examine the child and determine whether or not it should live.[1] This shows that the same arguments used to refute the humanness of the unborn child can be used as arguments against the humanness of a child who is already born. The issue is not when human life begins; the issue is whether or not human life is sacred.

Peter Singer, an ethics professor at Princeton University, acknowledges that unborn babies are human beings. However, he is consistent enough to acknowledge that the sanctity of human life principle only makes sense within the Judeo-Christian world view. Since Singer rejects this biblical world view, he is in favor of abortion on demand, and, if doctors and the baby's parents concur, infanticide of disabled newborn babies. Singer understands that if the God of the Bible does not exist, then human life is not sacred. Singer also promotes the "mercy-killing" of adult suffering patients who are conscious and want to die, as well as the euthanizing of unconscious patients who situations appear hopeless.[2]

The late Dr. Jerome Lejuene, the world renown geneticist who discovered Downs Syndrome, emphatically stated that medical science has proven that human life begins at the moment of conception.[3] At that instant, the unborn child has its complete genetic code, a unique blueprint for life which distinguishes it from its mother. Other medical experts such as Dr. Micheline M. Matthews-Roth and Dr. Hymie Gordon have also confirmed that human life begins at conception.[4] Since medical science has shown that human life begins at conception, abortion is the killing of an innocent human being.

There is much biblical evidence against abortion. King

David stated that he was sinful from the moment his mother conceived him (Psalm 51:5, NIV). Mere human "tissue" is not sinful; human beings are sinful. David was saying that he was a sinful human being from the moment of his conception. The Mosaic Law demanded the death penalty for causing the death of an unborn child (Exodus 21:22-25, NIV). The Bible refers to the fetus as "the babe in her womb" (Luke 1:41, 44). The Greek word for babe is "blephos," and it is used of infants both before and after birth (Luke 2:12).

The Bible teaches that since man was created in God's image, human life is sacred at any stage (Genesis 1:26-27; 9:6). Hence, the Bible forbids the taking of innocent life (Proverbs 6:16-19; Psalm 106:37-38). God alone is the giver of human life; He alone can rightfully take innocent human life (Job 1:21). Therefore, abortion—the killing of an unborn human child—is murder, the taking of an innocent life.

As we have seen, the debate is not about when human life begins, but whether human life is sacred. Pro-abortionists have decided that it is not. Partial-birth abortions only make more obvious the position that the leaders of this movement have always held—the view that unwanted human life can and should be terminated. The late Christian thinker Francis Schaeffer warned America that abortion would lead to infanticide (murder of infants already born) and euthanasia (so-called "mercy killing"). Partial-birth abortions have bridged the gap between abortion and infanticide. Human life has been devalued in this country. The extermination of the "undesirables" is in full swing.

As Christians, we are called to defend the helpless (James 1:27). Certainly, there is no one more helpless than an unborn child. Therefore, the church must stand up for the rights of the unborn. As the blood of Abel cried out from the ground for justice, so too the blood of millions of unborn babies cries out to a complacent church and calls her to action. The American holocaust must be stopped.

ENDNOTES

[1] Francis Schaeffer, *Complete Works*, vol. 5, (Westchester: Crossway Books, 1982), 231-235, 319-320.

[2] Peter Singer, *Practical Ethics*, second edition , (Cambridge: Cambridge University Press, 1993), 135-217, 342-343.

[3] R. C. Sproul, *Abortion, A Rational Look at an Emotional Issue* (Colorado Springs: NavPress, 1990), 159-191.

[4] Norman Geisler, *Christian Ethics* (Grand Rapids: Baker Book House, 1989), 149.

CHAPTER 18

THE BIBLICAL PERSPECTIVE CONCERNING HOMOSEXUALITY

by Phil Fernandes

W hat is the biblical perspective concerning homosexuality? The Bible unambiguously declares homosexuality to be a sin. Still, as Saint Augustine has written, we are to hate the sin, but love the sinner.[1] But, if we really love homosexuals, we will plead with them to flee from their lifestyles before it destroys them both physically and spiritually. A recent study which analyzed 7,500 obituaries revealed that the life expectancy of a homosexual male is forty-one years. The same study also uncovered that the life expectancy of heterosexual men who stayed married is seventy-five years. Other results of this study indicated that the life expectancy of lesbians is forty-four years, while women who stayed married have a life expectancy of seventy-nine years.[2] If we love smokers, we will plead with them to change their unhealthy lifestyles; should we not do the same for homosexuals?

Before we examine what the Bible says about homosexuality, we must keep in mind that the Scriptures do not consider homosexuality the only sexual sin. All sex outside of a monogamous marriage relationship between a man and a woman is declared by God to be sinful. Still, the focus of this chapter is homosexuality; therefore, I will now turn to what the Bible teaches concerning homosexuality.

THE BIBLICAL VIEW OF HOMOSEXUALITY

Genesis 1:27-28 tells us that God created mankind "male and female," and He commanded them to "multiply and fill the earth." Genesis 2:18 states that God decided to make for man a "helper suitable for him." Genesis 2:24 declares that a man "shall cleave to his wife; and they shall become one flesh." It is clear from these passages that the intention of God's creative purpose for human sexuality is a monogamous relationship between one man and one woman. Sexual intercourse within God's will is limited within the bonds of heterosexual, monogamous marriage. This conclusion is confirmed by our Savior Jesus Christ when He said, "Have you not read, that He who created them from the beginning made them male and female, and said, 'For this cause a man shall leave his father and his mother, and shall cleave to his wife; and the two shall become one flesh'" (Matthew 19:4-5).

The Bible tells us of the wickedness of Sodom and Gomorrah. Though homosexuality was not the only vice of these cities, the Bible makes it clear that this sin was one of the main reasons why God judged them. Genesis 19:1-11 speaks of the men of Sodom gathering at Lot's house and calling out to Lot, saying, "Where are the men who came to you tonight? Bring them out to us that we may have relations with them" (Genesis 19:5). Lot's two visitors were actually angels who manifested themselves as men. Lot's carnal attempt to rescue his visitors was his offer to provide the men of Sodom with his two virgin daughters (Genesis 19:8). But, the men of Sodom rejected Lot's offer. Finally, the angels miraculously struck the immoral men with blindness (Genesis 19:11). Jude, commenting on the destruction of Sodom and Gomorrah, wrote, "Just as Sodom and Gomorrah and the cities around them, since they in the same way as these indulged in gross immorality and went after strange flesh, are exhibited as an example, in undergoing the punishment of eternal fire" (Jude 7).

Leviticus 18:20-25 lists several sins that, if they become widespread in a society, will destroy that society. The sins listed include adultery, idolatry, infanticide, homosexuality, and bestiality. In this passage, God refers to homosexuality as an abomination. He states, "You shall not lie with a male as one lies with a female; it is an abomination" (Leviticus 18:22). God tells His chosen people that His judgment would fall upon the inhabitants of Canaan for practicing these vices; He warns Israel that His judgment will also fall on her if she partakes of the same sins. The Lord proclaims, "Do not defile yourselves by any of these things; for by all these the nations which I am casting out before you have become defiled. For the land has become defiled, therefore I have visited its punishment upon it, so the land has spewed out its inhabitants" (Leviticus 18:24-25). This passage should be viewed as a warning to all nations, both Jew and Gentile. As Dr. Tim Lahaye wrote in 1978, "A homosexually lenient society will incur the wrath of God."[3]

Under the Old Testament legal code, the Mosaic Law, the sin of homosexuality was punishable by death (Leviticus 20:13). However, Israel was a theocracy (ruled directly by God) and their religion was enforced by law. This is not the case in America. We are not God's chosen nation; we are a pluralistic society. Therefore, the death penalty for homosexual sins should probably not be enacted in Gentile countries. Still, the fact that God ordered the death penalty for the sin of homosexuality in Israel reveals clearly that God considers homosexuality a heinous offense.

The New Testament is as critical of the homosexual lifestyle as is the Old Testament. In Romans 1:18-32, the apostle Paul speaks of man's rejection of the true God, and the resulting descent into idolatry and gross immorality. Paul states that because men reject the true God, "God gave them over in the lusts of their hearts to impurity, that their bodies might be dishonored among them" (Romans 1:24). Paul declares, "For this reason God gave them over to degrading passions; for their women exchanged the natural function for that which is unnatural, and in the same way also the men abandoned the natural function of the woman and burned in their desire toward one another, men with men committing indecent acts and receiving in their own persons the due penalty of their error" (Romans 1:26-27). After listing several other sins, Paul proclaims, " . . . although they know the ordinance of God, that those who practice such things are worthy of death, they not only do the same, but also give hearty approval to those who practice them" (Romans 1:32). Paul's condemnation of homosexual desires is obvious, especially when one examines the descriptive terms he uses: lusts, impurity, and degrading passions. He refers to homosexual acts as unnatural and indecent. Paul's condemnation of homosexuality, in both thought and deed, is extremely clear. If a person accepts the Bible as God's Word, he or she should admit that homosexuality is one form of sinful rebellion against God.

The Bible's condemnation of homosexuality in 1 Corinthians 6:9-10 makes plain the fact that a person cannot be a practicing homosexual and a true believer at the same time. For Paul declares:

> Or do you not know that the unrighteous shall
> not inherit the kingdom of God? Do not be
> deceived; neither fornicators, nor idolaters, nor
> adulterers, nor effeminate, nor homosexuals, nor
> thieves, nor the covetous, nor drunkards, nor
> revilers, nor swindlers, shall inherit the kingdom
> of God (1 Corinthians 6:9-10).

Though a practicing homosexual is not a true believer, there is hope. For in the following verse Paul clearly teaches that a homosexual can be saved. Paul states, "And such were some of you; but you were washed, but you were sanctified, but you were justified in the name of the Lord Jesus Christ, and in the Spirit of our God" (1 Corinthians 6:11). The good news of the Gospel is that Jesus can save anyone who genuinely trusts in Him alone for salvation. However, Jesus saves us from both the penalty and the power of sin. Though true Christians are not perfect, their lives will be characterized by righteousness and good works. For God changes believers from within. Believers don't do good works to get saved; they do good works because they are saved (Ephesians 2:8-10; James 2:26; Romans 3:31). Both Jesus and Paul teach that true believers are no longer slaves to sin (John 8:31-36; Romans 6:17-18).

In 1 Corinthians 6:9-11, two Greek words are used to identify homosexuals. The first is "malakoi." This word means "those who are soft to the touch," and it is used of males who submit their bodies to unnatural sex acts performed by other males. The second word used for homosexuals in this passage is "arsenokoitai." This word means "one who lies with a male as with a female," "a sodomite," "a homosexual." These definitions are agreed upon by scholarly works such as *The New Thayer's Greek-English*

Lexicon,[4] and the Greek dictionaries of the *Strong's Concordance*[5] and *The New American Standard Exhaustive Concordance.*[6] Greek scholars such as A. T. Robertson[7] and Kenneth S. Wuest[8] also identify these words as terms denoting homosexuality.

There is also universal agreement among the leading Bible versions concerning these two Greek words found in 1 Corinthians 6:9-10. The major translations agree that these words denote homosexuality. The New American Standard Bible translates malakoi as "effeminate" and arsenokoitai as "homosexuals." The New King James Version translates malakoi as "homosexuals" and arsenokoitai as "sodomites." The New International Version translates malakoi as "male prostitutes" and arsenokoitai as "homosexual offenders." And, the King James Version translates malakoi as "effeminate," while translating arsenokoitai as "abusers of themselves with mankind."

In 1 Timothy 1:9-10, Paul again used the Greek word "arsenokoitai" for homosexuals. In this scripture, Paul refers to homosexuals and other sinners as "those who are lawless and rebellious." There is simply no way to honestly deny the fact that the Bible, both in the Old and New Testaments, declares homosexuality to be a gross sin. The biblical perspective concerning homosexuality is narrow and clear. The Bible calls homosexuality a sin.

Not only is outward homosexual behavior a sin, but the Bible also condemns homosexual desires. This was seen in Romans 1:24-27, where Paul denounced homosexual lusts as "degrading passions." Jesus agreed with Paul that sin originates in the heart of man (Matthew 23:25-28). Jesus stated, "but I say to you, that everyone who looks on a woman to lust for her has committed adultery with her already in his heart" (Matthew 5:28). Therefore, according to the Bible, sexual sins can occur in one's thoughts even if one does not partake of any sexually immoral behavior. This is why the Bible states that we need to be transformed by the renewing of our minds (Romans 12:2).

ARE HOMOSEXUAL TENDENCIES INHERITED?

Some proponents of homosexual rights claim that many people are born homosexuals; they had no choice in the matter. Homosexuality is viewed not as an acquired or learned behavior, but as something that is determined by a person's genetic makeup.[9] However, there is no undisputed evidence that homosexuality is genetically determined.[10] Many psychologists and psychiatrists who counsel homosexuals still view homosexuality as an acquired behavior.[11]

Several factors seem to discredit the notion that some people are born homosexual. For instance, many homosexuals have changed their lifestyles and become heterosexual.[12] But, how could this happen if they were genetically programmed to be homosexual? Also, there are many known cases where the identical twin of a homosexual is heterosexual. If homosexuality is genetically determined, this would not be the case.[13]

Still, even if we assume, for the sake of argument, that homosexual tendencies are genetic, this would change nothing. For the Bible teaches that all men inherit a sinful nature (Psalm 51:5). Because of our sinful nature, we naturally sin (Romans 3:10, 23). Still, the Bible holds us accountable for our sins and commands us to repent and turn to Jesus for the power to say no to sin (Mark 1:14-15; John 8:11, 31-36). Many infants are born addicted to nicotine or cocaine. But, we do not protect their right to smoke cigarettes or snort cocaine. Since we know these habits are unhealthy, we attempt to help them discard those destructive tendencies. If a man inherited a tendency towards violence, no one in their right mind would defend his right to beat people. If homosexuality is genetic, we would still be required to persuade the homosexual to flee this destructive lifestyle.

The good news of the Bible is that we can say yes to God and no to sin. Without Jesus, we are slaves to sin (John 8:31-36). But, with Jesus, we become new creations and slaves to righteousness (2 Corinthians 5:17; Romans 6:17-18). The homosexual who admits that he, like all men, is a sinner who cannot save himself, and genuinely turns to Jesus for forgiveness and salvation becomes a new creation. The Holy Spirit will indwell the former homosexual and empower him or her to flee from the destructive homosexual lifestyle.

The apostle Paul rejects the idea that a believer cannot refrain from giving in to temptation. He states:

> No temptation has overtaken you but such as is common to man; and God is faithful, who will not allow you to be tempted beyond what you are able, but with the temptation will provide the way of escape also, that you may be able to endure it (1 Corinthians 10:13).

Homosexuals can, as many have done, flee their sinful lifestyles by turning to Jesus for salvation. It is my earnest prayer that homosexuals would choose Jesus and reject their immoral lifestyles.

SHOULD HOMOSEXUALITY BE LEGAL?

We have shown that the Bible clearly calls homosexuality sinful. Now the question arises, "Should it be legal?" Americans live in a free country. This country does not enforce every detail of Christian morality. Still, the American concept of freedom is the freedom to pursue happiness, so long as one does not infringe on the freedom of another. Due to unhealthy practices such as anal intercourse (which is destructive to the body), the ingestion of feces (called rimming), the drinking of urine (called golden showers), and the insertion of one's fist into another's anus (called fisting),[14] homosexuality has become the breeding ground for many dangerous diseases. Some of these diseases (such as Hepatitis B and Tuberculosis) can be spread through casual contact.[15] Though AIDS apparently cannot be spread through casual contact, there are many homosexual diseases that can be spread this easily. Therefore, for the protection of society, homosexuality should be outlawed. Homosexuality is a public health issue; it is not a civil rights issue. We must never forget God's warning to Israel that widespread homosexuality will defile a nation (Leviticus 18:20-25).

Since God instituted human government to protect the well-being of its citizens (Romans 13:1-4), Christians are biblically justified in their attempts to return homosexuality to an illegal status. If homosexuality is not outlawed, America will become a diseased nation. This is not homophobia; it is theophobia, a healthy fear of God (Proverbs 1:7; Galatians 6:7).

Homosexuals need Jesus to save them from their sin. But, let us never forget that we are all sinners. Except for the grace of God, none of us would be saved. God's love drove His Son to Calvary to die a horrible death for our sins. Let us come to Jesus for salvation and forgiveness. Those who come to Him will not hunger, and those who believe in Him will never thirst (John 6:35).

ENDNOTES

[1] Saint Augustine, *City of God*, abridged, ed. Vernon J. Bourke (New York: Image Books, 1958), 304.

[2] "Homosexuality: A Lifestyle Leading to a Deathstyle," *National Liberty Journal*, February, 1995, 5.

[3] Tim LaHaye, *The Unhappy Gays* (Wheaton: Tyndale House Publishers, 1978), 201.

[4] *The New Thayer's Greek-English Lexicon* (Peabody: Hendrickson Publishers, 1981), 75, 387.

[5] *Strong's Exhaustive Concordance* (Iowa Falls: Riverside), "Greek Dictionary," 16, 46.

[6] *New American Standard Exhaustive Concordance* (Nashville: Holman Bible Publishers, 1981), "Greek Dictionary," 1635, 1664.

[7] A. T. Robertson, *Word Pictures in the New Testament*, vol. 4, (Grand Rapids: Baker Book House, 1931), 119.

[8] Kenneth S. Wuest, *Wuest's Word Studies From the Greek New Testament*, vol. 2, (Grand Rapids: William B. Eerdmans Publishing Company, 1970), 32 (2nd section). See also Kenneth S. Wuest, *The New Testament, An Expanded Translation* (Grand Rapids: William B. Eerdmans Publishing Company, 1984), 392.

[9] Roger Magnuson, *Informed Answers to Gay Rights Questions* (Sisters, Oregon: Multnomah, 1994), 81-90.

[10] Ibid., 83.

[11] William Dannemeyer, *Shadow in the Land* (San Francisco: Ignatius Press, 1989), 46-51.

[12] Magnuson, 84.

[13] Ibid.

[14] Gene Antonio, *The AIDS Cover-Up?* (San Francisco: Ignatius Press, 1986), 33-41.

[15] Ibid., 19-20, 44-45, 62-63, 99, 119-122.

CHAPTER 19

THE BIBLE CONDEMNS RACISM

by Phil Fernandes

U nfortunately, many racist groups deceive people by trying to claim a biblical basis for their hatred of races other than their own. These groups pull passages of the Bible totally out of their context and twist the true meaning of these passages to support their sinful racist ideologies. Some racist groups that make this absurd claim to be biblical are: "the Aryan Nations," "the Klu Klux Klan," "Neo-Nazism," "the Covenant," "the Sword," "the Arm of the Lord," and "the Order." These organizations are not Christian—there is absolutely no biblical support for their hatred of Jews, African-Americans, and other "non-white" races. The Bible does not teach that non-aryans are a "pre-Adamic race" or that the curse of Canaan is dark skin. These are misinterpretations of God's Word, fairy tales invented by warped minds in an attempt to give the appearance of divine sanction for sinful prejudices which have no place in the Gospel of our Lord Jesus Christ.

It should also be noted that racism can be found on both sides of the spectrum. "The Nation of Islam," headed by Louis Farakhan, perverts the teachings of the Islamic faith in order to justify this organization's anti-white and anti-Jewish rhetoric. Hence, racism is not limited to the white-against-black model; it can also be found in the black-against-white version. The sanctity of human life demands that we oppose racism in all its forms.

To set the record straight, we must look to the Bible for God's teaching on the matter. The Scriptures teach that all people were created in God's image (Genesis 1:26-27); therefore, all human life is sacred. All mankind is related— we are all descendants of Adam and Eve (Acts 17:26). The Bible teaches that even though mankind was created perfect, we fell into sin in the garden (Genesis 3), and, because of the Fall, we inherit a sin nature from our parents (Romans 5:12). Therefore, we are all sinners who need to be saved (Romans 3:10, 23; Matthew 19:25-26). The good news is that Jesus desires to save all mankind (Isaiah 45:22; 2 Peter 3:9; John 3:16-18; 14:6). Therefore, we should love all people regardless of their race or nationality (Matthew 5:43-47; Galatians 3:28).

Many people find it difficult to believe that America, a nation founded on Christian principles, once tolerated slavery based on race. Two points need to be addressed. First, America, as well as all of western culture, did not invent slavery; she inherited slavery. Slavery was not a Christian invention—it has been an evil human institution since mankind fell into sin in the Garden of Eden. Slavery was a direct result of man's sinfulness. Second, America and western culture, when they came of age and applied biblical principles to the question of slavery, put a stop to slavery. The abolitionist movements, both in America and Great

Britain, were almost completely comprised of Christians. In America, it took nearly 100 years for our country to begin to live consistently with our sacred belief that "all men are created equal." The writings of the founding fathers make it clear that the Declaration of Independence teaches that all of mankind (male or female, humans of every race and nationality) was created equal and that all humans are deserving of equal rights—God-given, inalienable rights. Hence, the Declaration of Independence and the US Constitution did not give a blank check of approval to slavery. Instead, these documents declared the death sentence on the institution of slavery. Though it took nearly 100 years for that death sentence to be carried out, the Christian principles found in these two documents formed the catalyst to crumble the edifice of slavery.

One further point needs to be made: no Christian should be anti-Jewish. Jesus, the apostles, the prophets, and the early church were all Jewish (John 4:22). In fact, all true Christians worship a Jewish carpenter, Jesus of Nazareth. The Bible teaches that Jesus will return to earth when all Israel is saved (Romans 11:25-27). Therefore, Christians should love the Jews and long to see them saved. Israel is still God's chosen nation.

Therefore, we cannot extend the hand of fellowship to churches in our community that promote racism. But we can plead with racists to turn to the true Creator, the God who created all of us and loves us so much that He sent His only son to die for us so that we could live forever.

CHAPTER 20

THE DANGERS OF PORNOGRAPHY

by Phil Fernandes

Pornography stores can be found throughout our country. Though many people believe that pornography is not harmful, I disagree. Both the Bible (the Word of God) and *The Final Report of the Attorney General's Commission on Pornography* (Rutledge Hill Press, 1986) discuss the dangers of pornography. There are several reasons why I believe pornography is wrong, even dangerous.

First, pornography is a sin. Jesus said that if a man looks at a woman to lust for her, he has committed adultery in his heart (Matthew 5:28). According to the Bible, a person does not have to outwardly act in order to sin; lustful thoughts are themselves sinful (Mark 7:20-23; James 1:14-15). A person can sin in his heart, as well as in his behavior. For this reason, the Apostle Paul tells us to let our minds dwell only on that which is true, honorable, right, pure, lovely, and worthy of praise (Philippians 4:8). What we choose to look at and think about will eventually effect our behavior (1 Samuel 11:1-4; Mark 7:20-23).

Second, pornography enslaves its customers. I have personally counseled several men who have become slaves to pornography. The Bible tells us that sin will master those who practice it (John 8:34). Paul wrote that we should "flee immorality" (1 Corinthians 6:18). Pornography is often a stumbling block that keeps a person from salvation in Jesus (Mark 9:42-48; John 3:19-21).

Third, pornography encourages a low level of respect for women. Pornography can warp a man's view of reality so that he begins to view women as mere sex objects, rather than as human beings created in God's image (Genesis 1:26-27).

Fourth, pornography victimizes women. I am convinced that the high rate of sexual harassment, divorce, unwed mothers, and rape can be traced to a low view of women. As noted above, this low view of women is fostered by pornography.

Fifth, pornography arouses a person's sexual appetite; it does not satisfy his or her sexual appetite. Once sexually aroused by pornography, how will the customer satisfy his or her sexual desires? At best, pornography helps to produce a sexually promiscuous and irresponsible society. At worst, in extreme though not rare cases, pornography has led some of its customers to rape and murder others in an attempt to quench their uncontrollable sexual thirsts.

Sixth, in most cases, pornography supports organized crime. Crime families from Chicago, New York, New Jersey, and Florida control and oversee the pornography business in Los Angelos. In 1975, organized crime controlled 80% of America's pornography industry. Today, law enforcement experts believe that organized crime controls over 90% of this industry.

I believe that Christians must uncompromisingly preach against all sin, including pornography, and that local governments should seriously consider outlawing pornography because of its detrimental effects on communities. However, for those who are enslaved by pornography, Christians must offer hope. Though everyone who habitually sins is a slave of that sin, Jesus will set free any captive who turns from his or her sin and comes to Him for deliverance (John 8:34, 36).

CHAPTER 21

SAVE THE WHALES?

by Phil Fernandes

SECULAR HUMANISM AND THE ENVIRONMENT

Should we pollute, worship, or preserve our planet? A person's world view should help him answer this question.

The atheistic world view, in its optimistic form, is called secular humanism. As *Humanist Manifestos I* and *II* proclaim, secular humanists believe that mankind can save this planet without help from God. Through technology, education, and the socialistic redistribution of wealth, we will save the planet earth from destruction.

However, if atheism is true and there is no God and no life after death, then why should we care about saving the planet? If the atheist responds to this question by saying that we should try to help future generations of humans, then our response is twofold. First, from an atheistic perspective, why should we even care about future generations? After all, human life loses its sacredness if there is no God. Second, even future generations will eventually die out—the human race is only a temporary accident in the history of a meaningless universe (if atheism is true). If the day will come when mankind will be no more, then why even fight for future generations?

The apostle Paul said it best: "If the dead are not raised, let us eat and drink for tomorrow we die" (1 Corinthians 15:32). Atheism, if consistently applied to one's life, leads to selfishness, and selfishness does not motivate humans to protect the environment.

THE NEW AGE MOVEMENT AND THE ENVIRONMENT

The New Age pantheistic world view teaches that the universe is God and, since living things are part of the universe, living things are divine. Hence, New Agers worship the earth. They protest to save endangered species (whales, wolves, seals, spotted owls, etc.), to fight pollution, and to save the planet (Gaia the earth goddess).

The Christian response to New Age radical environmentalism is sixfold. First, there is a God, but we are not Him! The worship of creation is idolatry and the worship of self is blasphemy; it is the lie Satan told Eve in the Garden. Second, saving seals and whales, but not unborn babies, is inconsistent. If all of creation is God, then New Agers should be opposed to killing any living thing. New Agers are often vegetarians—they refuse to eat meat. Other New Agers are slightly more consistent—they refuse to eat dairy products and meat, for a slice of cheese is as divine as a cow. Still, if New Agers lived consistently with their beliefs they would also refrain from eating vegetables (which, in the New Age view, are also divine). In short, consistent New Agers would starve to death.

Third, the New Age/pantheistic belief in reincarnation

leads to neglect of suffering people (as evidenced in India). For if we help alleviate someone's sufferings, then we retard his reincarnation cycle and postpone his escape from reincarnation—the attainment of nirvana, becoming one with the world soul. Consistent pantheism allows people to suffer in order to work off their negative karma in this life so they won't have to suffer for it in a future life.

Fourth, the New Age movement, although it calls man "god," has a low view of human life. Ironically, most New Agers reject the sanctity of human life. Leading New Agers like Barbara Marx Hubbard teach that we should terminate the existence of humans who hold back the coming New Age of spiritual enlightenment. Just as dead branches are removed from a tree to enhance the growth of the tree, so too must undesirable humans be removed.

Fifth, New Agers are usually socialists or communists. Either way, they are opposed to people owning private property. But history has shown that people tend to treat their own property with more respect than the property of others. Therefore, the abolition of private property would help destroy the earth rather than save it. An obvious example of this is the cow. There are probably more cows killed than any other animal, because Americans like steak. Still, cows are not an endangered species. Ranchers who own the cows see to it that their cows reproduce at a higher rate than the rate of cows being slaughtered. Since they own the cows and the cows are essential to their livelihoods, the ranchers do everything in their power to increase the size of their herds. On the other hand, Marxist regimes in Africa do not allow their citizens to own elephants. This encourages pouching, and this endangers the future of the elephant.

Sixth, New Age radical environmentalism is based on pseudo-science. Radical environmentalism ultimately is a tool of wanna-be tyrants who wish to enslave the masses by abolishing private property. It has no basis in honest scientific investigation (see Michael S. Coffman's *Saviors of the Earth*, published by Northfield Publishers).

CHRISTIANITY AND THE ENVIRONMENT

As Christians, we should not worship the earth, nor pollute it. Though God gave man dominion over the earth (Genesis 1:27-28), man is accountable to God—we should be faithful stewards over all that God has entrusted to us (1 Timothy 4:4-5; Genesis 2:15; 1 Corinthians 4:2). Still, our treatment of the earth should be based upon true science, not political correctness or Marxist ideology.

The earth belongs to the Lord (Job 41:11; Psalm 50:12; 104:10-14). Therefore, we should treat it with respect. In biblical times, the Jews were an example of being faithful stewards of God's creation. Rather than destroying the land, the Jews rested the land when it needed to be rejuvenated (Exodus 23:10-11).

The earth is not God, but it is a gift of God. Therefore, we need to be faithful stewards of the earth.

POSTSCRIPT: DO ANIMALS HAVE RIGHTS?

Rights entail moral responsibilities; animals are not morally responsible; hence, animals do not have rights. We do not arrest and imprison a lion for brutally killing another lion. Lions, as are all non-human animals, are creatures of instinct; they are not free moral agents. Therefore, animals do not have rights.

Humans have rights because we were created in God's image, and that entails being moral beings. Rights always come with responsibilities—we are held accountable for our actions.

Still, we should treat animals appropriately. Just because animals do not have rights does not mean that we can kill or torture them for fun. Animals are gifts to man from God, and we should never treat them harshly because of this. God gave man permission to kill and eat animals (Genesis 9:1-5). He did not give man permission to torture, kill, and waste animals. All of God's creation should be treated with the appropriate respect simply because it *is* God's creation. We should never take for granted the gifts God has given us.

CHAPTER 22

"WHOEVER SHEDS MAN'S BLOOD . . ."

by Phil Fernandes

It is rather ironic that many people who have no problem killing unborn and newly born babies devote their lives to protecting the lives of cold-blooded serial murderers. In fact, it is even common to find Christians arguing to save the "precious" life of a Ted Bundy or a John Wayne Gasey. Christians need to understand that though the Bible speaks of forgiveness and love, it also speaks of justice. While the church should be in the business of grace, mercy, love, and forgiveness, God instituted the government to execute justice.

Much confusion stems from Jesus' statement in Matthew 5 concerning the "eye for an eye" principle. Jesus declared, "You have heard that it was said, 'An eye for an eye, and a tooth for a tooth.' But I say to you, do not resist him who is evil; but whoever slaps you on your right cheek, turn to him the other also" (Matthew 5:38-39).

The first thing we need to note about this passage is that Jesus is questioning something that was "said," not something that was written. In other words, Jesus is not rejecting the "eye for an eye" principle of Exodus 21:23-25; rather, He is refuting the faulty spoken tradition of the Jewish rabbis of His day. These rabbis twisted the Exodus 21 passage out of its proper context. Rather than acknowledging that the "eye for an eye" principle applied to the government as the arbiter of justice, they applied this passage to the personal lives of Jews, thus giving their approval to the taking of personal revenge. Jesus was saying that it is wrong to take revenge; He was not telling the governing authorities to forgive premeditated murderers. This is consistent with Paul's teaching that Christians are not to take their own revenge, but the government was instituted by God to punish evildoers (Romans 12:17-21; 13:1-4).

Second, the "eye for an eye" principle is a poetic way of saying "justice." All it means is that the punishment is to fit the crime. That is what justice (i.e., fairness) is all about. It would be unethical for a government to sentence a ruthless murderer to seven years in prison. Yet, that is what our country does time and time again.

Third, the Bible recognizes the individual's right to self-defense (Exodus 22:2-4; Luke 22:36-38). But, once the person is out of imminent danger, the victim is commanded to turn the matter over to the governing authorities rather than taking his own revenge.

Therefore, Jesus was speaking against the taking of personal vengeance; He was not opposing the government's exercising capital punishment. Individual Christians should practice forgiveness, but that is not the case with the governing authorities. They are commanded by God to execute justice.

Some Christians argue that the "eye for an eye" principle, since it is part of the Mosaic Law, no longer applies today. However, when they assume this they fail to realize that God delegated His authority to execute murderers to human governments immediately after the global flood. This was long before the start of the Jewish nation and the establishment of the Mosaic Law. Noah was the father of all nations (Jew and Gentile). Immediately after giving permission for man to kill and eat animals, God told Noah that "Whoever sheds man's blood, by man his blood shall be shed. For in the image of God He made man" (Genesis 9:6). Hence, God commanded all governments (Jew and Gentile) to execute murderers, and the reason for this is the sanctity of human life (Genesis 1:26-27). Because man was created in God's image, human life is sacred. Capital punishment promotes the sanctity of human life by executing those who take innocent human life. It also deters violent crime by giving the would-be murderer less incentive to commit the crime. He who sheds innocent blood (commits murder) forfeits his own right to life.

The Bible also teaches that the retribution for crime should come quickly in order to deter future crimes (Ecclesiastes 8:11). Our present appeals process, which often takes over a decade in murder cases, directly contradicts this biblical principle. It seems that the legal system in this country has more concern for the "rights" of the criminal than it does for the rights of the victim. State governments must decide whether they will protect the criminal or the law-abiding citizen, for it is impossible to protect both. God instituted human government to protect the law-abiding citizen and to punish the evil-doer; one would not know that from watching our courts in action.

One final issue is that of the rehabilitation of criminals. Simply put, it is not biblical. God ordained human government to bring retribution upon a criminal, not to rehabilitate the criminal. Criminals are not sick people who need to be healed; they are evil people who need to be punished. They are evil by choice. It is the church's job to lead people to Christ and disciple them. It is the church's job to encourage people, even criminals, to allow the Holy Spirit to transform their lives. But it is the government's job to punish the criminal, not to counsel or rehabilitate him.

Christians need to evangelize and disciple murderers on death row. But we must allow the government to do its job, for "whoever sheds man's blood, by man his blood shall be shed."

CHAPTER 23

CIVIL DISOBEDIENCE AND REVOLUTION

by Phil Fernandes

CIVIL DISOBEDIENCE

The Bible clearly commands us to submit to the governing authorities (Romans 13:1-7; 1 Peter 2:13-17). However, Paul and Peter were both put to death for civil disobedience, for they disobeyed the government by continuing to preach the Gospel. Thousands of early Christians followed their example by being martyred for the Faith. When ordered to stop preaching about Jesus, the apostles told the Sanhedrin, "we must obey God rather than men" (Acts 5:29). When we are forced to choose between obeying a law of human government and the will of God, we must choose to obey God, acknowledging His law as a higher law.

Rahab the Harlot refused to submit to the governing authorities of Canaan. She refused to reveal to the Canaanite governing authorities the whereabouts of the two innocent Jewish spies (Joshua 2). In fact, she actively lied to these authorities and hid the spies. She understood that saving innocent human life was of higher importance than submitting to human government and telling the truth. God complements Rahab for her act of civil disobedience (Hebrews 11:31; James 2:25). When God's laws and man's laws conflict (i.e., when we cannot obey both) it is the greater good to obey God's laws.[1]

The Hebrew midwives Shiphrah and Puah refused to kill newborn Israelite babies even though they had been ordered to do so by the Egyptian Pharoah (Exodus 1). They also lied to the governing authorities to protect these innocent babies. Again, God's Word commends them for their actions.

Therefore, though the Bible commands us to submit to the governing authorities, our submission to God is of greater importance. When we cannot obey both God and the government, we must obey God.

A current example of this is found in Communist China. China's one-child-per-family policy forces families who already have one child to abort any other babies conceived. In many cases the pregnant woman will resist the government and try to bring her second (or third, etc.) child to term and raise the child in defiance of the communist regime. God is pleased when people place themselves at risk to protect the innocent lives of other human beings.

It should also be noted that though the Bible commands us to submit to the governing authorities, it does not tell us to have blind faith in our government officials. God's Word tells us "It is better to take refuge in the Lord than to trust in man. It is better to take refuge in the Lord than to trust in princes" (Psalm 118:8-9). Blind patriotism is not biblical. We should be good citizens and try to elect godly men and women to office, but we should not blindly trust them. Government officials are just as fallen as we are. The idea that American politicians are immune to lusting for power and would never betray the constitution, our country, or our people is not a Christian idea. We need to take the Fall of mankind seriously and remember that every human government, given enough time, will eventually go bad.

So it is clear that there are times when the Bible encourages disobedience. But, what about revolution? The Bible declares that all government has been ordained by God. Does this mean that revolution is never justified?

REVOLUTION AND JUST WAR

Some Christian thinkers like philosopher Norman Geisler believe the founding fathers were not justified when they revolted against Great Britain.[2] Other Christian thinkers like Francis Schaeffer believe the American Revolution was a just war.[3] Before we can decide if revolution is ever justified, we must answer the question of whether or not any war is justified.

Christians scholars have arrived at what is referred to as the "just war doctrine." This teaching expounds upon the list of factors needed to deem a war just. The just war doctrine is as follows. First, there must be a just cause or sufficient reason to engage in war (i.e., self-defense, protect innocent human life, safeguard human rights, etc.). Second, the war must be declared by competent authority (i.e., the government, not private groups). Third, the principle of comparative justice says that one's nation must be more just than the other nation involved in the war. Fourth, a just war is fought with the right intention in mind. In other words, there must be a desire for peace, a restraining of evil, and an assisting of the good. Fifth, engaging in war should only be as a last resort—all peaceful alternatives should be exhausted before war is undertaken. Sixth, there must be a probability of success. Though it is impossible to be completely certain about the outcome of a war, a nation should not knowingly shed blood in vain. Seventh, the principle of proportionality means that the good to be achieved by war must outweigh the evil that will result from the war. And, eighth, the principle of discrimination declares that innocent civilians should not be targeted; only combatants and legitimate military targets should be pursued.[4]

Two furthers points need to be stressed. First, even if a war is just, it must still be fought justly. The fact that a nation has engaged in a just war does not relieve that nation from the responsibility of fighting the war in a just manner.[5] Second, the Bible is clear that a God-ordained war overrides the just war criteria, for as the Giver of life, only God has the right to take "innocent" life (Job 1:21). Therefore, He can order His people to slay every man, woman, and child and that war would still be just (Deuteronomy 20:16-18; Joshua 10:40). Therefore, the just war doctrine applies to human governments, but not to God.

When the just war doctrine is applied to the American revolution, it is my opinion that our founding fathers were justified in revolting against Great Britain, for their rights were being infringed upon and the colonists had exhausted all peaceful means. The revolution was waged by competent authority since lower level magistrates led the revolt against Great Britain and the higher ranked officials.

It is interesting to note that when one applies the principle of competent authority to America's wars, all wars after World War II are called into question. For the U.S. Constitution gives the only authority to declare war to the U.S. Congress, but all wars after World War II were fought under the authority of the United Nations. The U.S. Constitution gives absolutely no authority whatsoever to any international body. Fighting communism is a good thing. Our veterans from Vietnam, Korea, and the Persian Gulf are true heroes. Still, we must hold our leaders accountable—they are not doing their jobs when they give the reigns of this country to an international body like the UN. Our founding fathers had a word for this; they called it treason.

Returning to the subject of revolution, obviously it is not something that should be engaged in lightly. The right to revolt should only be exercised as a last resort. The principle of self-defense is applicable at this point. God instituted human government to protect people and their God-given rights. When the government actually becomes the greatest threat to people's safety, the people always have the God-given right to defend themselves.

It is my prayer that the US government never reaches that point. However, once the battle of words has been lost and the debate is over, if America ever enslaves its people and begins to execute Christians and lovers of freedom, due to modern weaponry and technology, all that will remain is the right to protect oneself and one's family in small groups of resistance. Though we should pray that God will spare us, all human governments eventually go bad. I am of the opinion that America is on the downward slide and her collapse may even be imminent. Still, I hope that I am wrong. I hope that the blood shed to win and keep our freedom was not shed in vain.

ENDNOTES

[1] Norman L. Geisler, *Christian Ethics* (Grand Rapids: Baker Book House, 1989), 113-132.

[2] Ibid., 248-255.

[3] Francis A. Schaeffer, *A Christian Manifesto* (Westchester: CrossWay Books, 1981).

[4] Geisler,233-234. Joseph P. Martino, *A Fighting Chance: The Moral Use of Nuclear Weapons* (San Francisco: Ignatius Press, 1988), 106-107.

[5] Geisler, 234.

CHAPTER 24

THE ETHICS OF NUCLEAR DEFENSE

by Phil Fernandes

Many well-meaning Christians are opposed to the U.S. military's building and maintaining a strong nuclear defense. In the 1980's, Roman Catholic Archbishop Raymond Hunthausen argued that the United States should unilaterally disarm her nuclear defense. He believed that this would further the cause of world peace. Having once disarmed, reasoned Hunthausen, if we are invaded, we should bear our cross by surrendering to our captors. Apparently, the Archbishop agreed with British atheist Bertrand Russell who once said, "better red than dead."

However, common sense and biblical principles tell a different story. For weakening the earth's strongest free nation does not in any way further the cause of world peace. In fact, it does the opposite—it leaves the rest of the world at the mercy of totalitarian regimes. If the strongest nation on earth is a free nation, then this nation could be a roadblock to the spread of tyranny.[1]

The research of R. J. Rummel has shown that, in the twentieth century, dictatorships have murdered more of their own people (over 120 million) during peace time than the number of people who have died in wars throughout the history of mankind.[2] Therefore, appeasing tyrannical regimes does not serve the purpose of world peace; it invites the enslavement and slaughter of millions.

It is clear that America should build a strong nuclear defense, but a deterrent is not a defense. In the Carter administration, our nuclear weapons strategy was called "Mutually Assured Destruction" (MAD). This strategy encouraged a balance of nuclear power between the United States and her leading enemy, the Soviet Union. In this program, cities of both countries were targeted as a threat. It was thought that, if there were nuclear exchanges, the United States and the Soviet Union would destroy each other. Supposedly, this would be enough to deter both countries from starting a nuclear war.

Retired U.S. Air Force Colonel Joseph Martino has persuasively argued that the "Mutually Assured Destruction" policy is severely flawed.[3] First, if the bluff fails and the Soviet Union (now Russia) initiates a nuclear war with a first strike, the choice left to our leaders would be either suicide (by retaliating) or surrender. Second, the United States currently values the lives of its citizens more than Russia. Hence, Russia may be willing to sacrifice millions of citizens in return for military conquest. Third, a deterrent is not a defense; it is merely a bluff, and if our bluff is called, we are not prepared to win a nuclear war.

Former President Ronald Reagan opposed the deterrent strategy and sought to produce a true nuclear defense.[4] This meant that America would have the capability of winning a nuclear war, if necessary. A nuclear defense would entail the production of smaller, mobile, and more accurate nuclear weapons. With the smaller missiles there would be less radioactive fall-out; hence, less loss of innocent life. Keeping the nuclear missiles mobile would make it extremely difficult for enemy forces to target them in a nuclear first strike. Since more of our nuclear offensive would survive an enemy first strike, our retaliation could devastate the enemy's military. (This stresses the importance of the Trident nuclear subs, which are mobile; hence, their changing locations are not easily detected.) The greater accuracy would enable the U.S. to target and hit strategic military targets, rather than the targeting of cities and the killing of thousands of non-combatants (which would violate the just war criteria of Christian tradition).

Martino points out that Ronald Reagan also wanted a true defense against a nuclear attack. This was called the "Star Wars Defense System."[5] This system, if produced, would give the United States military the ability to shoot and destroy incoming nuclear warheads. Professor Robert Jastrow, astrophysicist and founder of NASA's Institute for Space Studies, has argued that, using 1980's smart-bullet technology and heat-sensitive detectors, the U.S. could construct a four layered missile defense system that would destroy 998 out of every 1,000 nuclear warheads targeting our nation.[6] Jastrow adds that the advances of laser technology would only increase the accuracy of a missile defense.[7]

With the ability to wage and win a nuclear war, and a missile defense system in place, the U.S. military could greatly reduce the chance of nuclear war occurring. Tyrannical regimes would not be likely to initiate a nuclear war knowing their chances of winning were non-existent.

Being a peacemaker is not merely the petitioning of governments to reduce their nuclear arsenals. Being a peacemaker entails real solutions to real problems. The cause of war and innocent bloodshed is not the production of inanimate weapons. The cause is the evil heart of fallen man, and, because of man's sinfulness, free countries need to build strong defenses. War is inevitable; it is a product of the Fall. The question remains, "Will America be prepared when the next war begins?"

ENDNOTES

[1] This is not to say that the United States has the responsibility or the right to be the "policeman" of the world. However, the keeping of peace within our borders and the protecting of American interests around the globe would certainly make the world a safer place to live.

[2] R. J. Rummel, *Death by Government* (New Brunswick: Transaction Publishers, 1994), 1-28. See also The *Black Book of Communism* (Cambridge, Massachusetts: Harvard University Press, 1999).

[3] Joseph P. Martino, *A Fighting Chance: The Moral Use of Nuclear Weapons* (San Francisco: Ignatius Press, 1988).

[4] Ibid., 91-92.

[5] Ibid., 230-245.

[6] Robert Jastrow, *How To Make Nuclear Weapons Obsolete* (Boston: Little, Brown, and Company, 1985), 113-114.

[7] Ibid., 83-88, 41-43.

CHAPTER 25

A CHRISTIAN PHILOSOPHY OF EDUCATION

by Phil Fernandes

THE JUDEO-CHRISTIAN VIEW OF EDUCATION

The biblical or Judeo-Christian philosophy of education is the traditional view of education. In this perspective, it is the parents' responsibility to educate their children (Proverbs 22:6; Deuteronomy 4:9; Ephesians 6:4). The parents may choose to directly educate their children or they may decide to delegate that responsibility to another person (or other persons). But God holds the parents responsible for raising their children in the truth of God's Word. For this reason, parents should not send their children to non-believing teachers using a non-Christian (or anti-Christian) curriculum.

The Bible says that the non-believer considers the

Gospel foolishness and that he cannot understand God's truths (1 Corinthians 1:18; 2:14). This is because the non-believer has been blinded by Satan (2 Corinthians 4:3-4). Jesus said that if the teachers are spiritually blind, their students will also be spiritually blind (Luke 6:39-40), for the spiritually blind will lead their students astray. Can we Christians biblically justify sending our children to the spiritually blind for an education? Obviously, the answer is no.

God's Word tells us that we are not to be unequally yoked with the world, for we have no fellowship with the darkness of the world (2 Corinthians 6:14-18). Therefore, Christians should not send their children to the unsaved world for an education. Education cannot be taught in a moral or spiritual vacuum; the curriculum will either be Christian or anti-Christian. It cannot be neutral.

THE WORLD'S VIEW OF EDUCATION

The Greek philosopher Plato (4th century BC) believed that it was the job of the state to educate the children, and that the state could produce an ideal society through its education program. Plato reasoned that the state is better equipped than the parents to raise children. Hence, the state was responsible for selecting the future careers of the children. Obviously, these powers would inevitably lead to an all-powerful state (tyranny).

In the 19th century, Karl Marx, the founder of communism, argued that the family unit should be abolished, and that the state should raise and educate the children. Marx saw free education for all as a way to indoctrinate children in communism, and he viewed Christianity as something harmful to children.

In the 20th century, John Dewey, "the father of modern education," declared that the state should educate the children. He was a socialist who saw the public schools as a way to indoctrinate the children in socialism. He believed that education should be less theoretical and more practical, thus teaching children to be productive workers in society who do not have the knowledge to refute their socialistic rulers. Dewey, like Marx, was an atheist who believed that traditional religion was detrimental to a child's development. Dewey was a signer of the 1933 *Humanist Manifesto*, the most renowned atheist document of its day.

THE FOUNDING FATHERS' VIEW OF EDUCATION

America's founding fathers held to the Judeo-Christian view of education. They knew that the parents would have their children's best interests in heart and would be best suited for educating their children or entrusting others to educate their children. The founding fathers knew that, if the federal government had any say in the education of children, it would abuse that power and use education as a tool to indoctrinate the students in political correctness. This is why the U.S. Constitution gives absolutely no power to the federal government to educate the children, and the 10th amendment to the Constitution declares that any power not clearly given to the federal government in the Constitution falls back to the people and the individual states. Therefore, the current control of the public schools by the federal government is unconstitutional.

THE CURRENT SITUATION

Today, the U.S. Constitution is being ignored. The founding fathers' view of education (the biblical view of education) has been replaced by the world's view of education as espoused by Plato, Marx, and Dewey. The federal government is indoctrinating children in political correctness, rather than educating them. Christianity has been kicked out of the public schools, while atheistic evolution and new age paganism are being proclaimed to impressionable young minds.

The state of public education is depressing. Through

UNESCO (United Nations Education, Scientific, and Cultural Organization), the United Nations is influencing students in America and throughout the world. Outcome Based Education, Goals 2000, and America 2000 train children to renounce any loyalty to America and teach them to become global citizens. Muticulturalism slanders Christianity, western culture, and the founding fathers, while at the same time it glorifies earth-worshiping cultures. Through "values clarification," children are taught moral relativism, the denial of universal rights and wrongs.

As public school SAT scores continue to plummet, private schools and home schooling are becoming extremely popular options. Unfortunately, they should have been the only options. For God never intended an all-powerful state to indoctrinate children in anti-Christian propaganda. Instead, He commanded parents to bring up their children in His wisdom and ways. If we care for our children, we will obey the Lord's command.

CHAPTER 26

IF THE BLIND LEAD THE BLIND . . .

by Phil Fernandes

On October 31, 1935, more than twenty-five years before prayer was taken out of the public schools, the late Christian thinker Gordon Clark gave a speech stressing the need for Christian education. Clark warned that public education, in its attempt to be non-Christian, would become anti-Christian. Clark stated that "education is . . . the responsibility of the family," and that "it is primarily to parents . . . that God has entrusted the children and their upbringing." He added that "there are powerful forces at work in the world and in these United States to destroy the family and to make children, yes and adults too, the creatures of the State."[1]

Clark saw the centralization of authority in the public school system leading America down the path towards a dictatorship that would use its power "to destroy the family and to exalt the state." He argued that public education was fast becoming a "means of political propaganda."[2]

Clark knew that the Church and the world have different ideas as to what constitutes a good education. The Church believes that education must include moral and spiritual preparation essential to godly living. The world rejects the authority of the God of the Bible and encourages children to accept the "new morality" (i.e., a sinful lifestyle). Clark also recognized that the state would abuse its power and indoctrinate children, molding them into adults who would gladly and mindlessly accept their servitude before the presence of a totalitarian regime.[3]

Obviously, Clark was a man before his time, a thinker who could foresee, decades in advance, the future consequences of the anti-Christian ideas that began to permeate the American public school system of his day. He was also a patriotic American who agreed with the founding fathers of this nation and the constitution they authored. Clark saw that the federal government had no right to control public education, and that, if it did, the schools would become centers of indoctrination in political correctness, rather than centers of genuine learning. It was Karl Marx who believed that the government should educate the children rather than their parents; it was also Karl Marx who called for the abolition of the family.[4]

Today, we see that Gordon Clark was right. Currently, *Goals 2000* and *Outcome Based Education* are being taught to America's children, training them to be global citizens and to reject the moral values of their parents. *Multiculturalism* (curriculum designed to slander Western culture, Christianity, and our founding fathers) and *sex education* (pro-homosexual indoctrination) work to tear children from the values taught them by their parents.[5]

In 1972, thirty-seven years after Clark's speech, Harvard University Professor Chester M. Pierce gave the keynote address to the Association for Childhood Education International. He stated that "every child in America entering school . . . is insane because he comes to school with certain allegiances toward our founding fathers, toward his parents, toward a belief in a supernatural being . . . It's up to you, teachers, to make all of these sick children well—by creating the international children of the future."

In 1935, Gordon Clark pleaded with the Church to recognize the threat of public education, and called upon Christian parents to build Christian schools for the purpose of bringing up their children "in the discipline and instruction of the Lord" (Ephesians 6:4). If we do not heed the warning of Gordon Clark—if we turn our children over to the anti-Christian state to be educated—then our children will suffer the consequences. For our Savior said, "A blind man cannot guide a blind man, can he? Will they not both fall into a pit? A pupil is not above his teacher; but everyone, after he has been fully trained, will be like his teacher." (Luke 6:39-40).

ENDNOTES

[1] Gordon Clark, *A Christian Philosophy of Education* (Jefferson: The Trinity Foundation, 1988), 205.

[2] Ibid.

[3] Ibid., 200-201.

[4] Karl Marx and Friedrich Engels, *The Communist Manifesto*.

[5] William Norman Grigg, *Freedom on the Altar* (Appleton: American Opinion Publishing, 1995), 50-54.

CHAPTER 27

DOES PHILOSOPHY REALLY MAKE A DIFFERENCE?

By Phil Fernandes

═══════════════════

People often relegate philosophers to academic lecture halls that have no contact with the real world. Philosophy is commonly viewed as dealing merely with the abstract world of ideas, not real life issues that confront the "average person." In this article, the question of whether or not philosophy makes a difference will be addressed. A sample of Friedrich Nietzsche's philosophical views will be discussed to ascertain the effect, if any, on the generations that followed him.

Friedrich Nietzsche (1844-1900) was a German philosopher who proclaimed that "God is dead."[1] By this he meant that mankind had once created God through wishful thinking.[2] Later, the human race intellectually matured to the point where God was seen to be non-existent. "Intellectuals" throughout the world were beginning to embrace atheism as their world-view, and Christianity was no longer the dominant world view of western culture.

But Nietzsche saw a contradiction in the thought of these "intellectuals." Though he agreed with their atheism, he rejected their acceptance of traditional moral values. Nietzsche argued that since God is dead, traditional values have died with Him.[3] If the God of the Bible does not exist, reasoned Nietzsche, then the moral values taught in the Bible have no hold over mankind.

Nietzsche redefined the good as "the will to power."[4] He called for a group of "supermen" to arise with the boldness to create their own values.[5] He proposed that these "supermen" replace the "soft values" of Christianity with what he called "hard values."[6]

Nietzsche predicted that man would come of age. By this he meant that the atheist of the twentieth century would realize the consequences of a world without God. For without God there are no absolute moral values. Man is free to play God and create his own morality. Because of this, prophesied Nietzsche, the twentieth century would be the bloodiest century in human history.[7]

The writings of Friedrich Nietzsche, far from being irrelevant to real life issues, influenced the thought of many people. One person affected by the thought of Nietzsche was Adolph Hitler. Nietzsche's call for the rise to power of the supermen became the rallying cry for the master race of Nazism. Approximately six million Jews were barbarically murdered. Nietzsche himself detested anti-Semitism. Still, had Nietzsche been alive during Hitler's reign, he would have had no basis to judge the actions of the supermen "evil." For Nietzsche's philosophy was one totally void of moral absolutes. Once God is removed and man is given the power to arbitrarily create his own moral values, man is free to do as he pleases.

Does philosophy really make a difference? In the case of Friedrich Nietzsche, the answer is yes. The moral relativism he proclaimed, the supermen he called for, and the hard values he desired were instrumental in leading to the holocaust and World War II. Millions have suffered due to a racist ideology that looked to Nietzsche's work for its rational justification. Though the effects of one's philosophy are rarely this catastrophic, there is often a direct correlation between the ideas of leading philosophers and the course of human history.

The world abounds with anti-Christian philosophies. If the Church remains silent and these philosophies are not refuted, what will befall mankind in the twenty-first century?

ENDNOTES

[1] *The Portable Nietzsche*, ed. Walter Kaufman (New York: Penguin Books, 1968), 124, 447.

[2] Ibid., 143, 198.

[3] Norman L. Geisler and Paul D. Feinberg, *Introduction to Philosophy* (Grand Rapids: Baker Book House, 1980), 408.

[4] *The Portable Nietzsche*, 570.

[5] Geisler and Feinberg, 408.

[6] Ibid.

[7] Frederick Copleston, *A History of Philosophy*, vol. VII (New York: Doubleday, 1963), 405-406.

CHAPTER 28

A GOLDEN CALF IN THE CITY OF GOD?

by Phil Fernandes

While Moses was on the mountain receiving God's Law, the Israelite people grew restless. Rather than waiting on the Lord, they persuaded Aaron to build a golden calf for them that they might worship it (Exodus 32).

Today, God's church—what Saint Augustine called "the City of God"—is not beyond worshiping golden calves. Many contemporary evangelical leaders are leading their flocks to trust in non-Christian ideologies (the wisdom of man) to solve their problems. Even leaders can stray; they are not beyond sin. We must never forget that Aaron was the high priest of the Jewish nation, the chosen people of God. Still, he took part in the idolatry.

The evangelical church stood firm against attacks from secular humanism, theological liberalism, and neo-orthodoxy. Unfortunately, the enemy has slipped into God's camp unnoticed. There is a golden calf—a false idol—in the church today. It brings with it a false hope as it destroys the lives of many.

This contemporary idol is not a statue made of gold; it is an ideology that is leading Christians astray. This idol is secular psychology, and it takes one's focus off Christ and places it on one's self.

The Bible teaches that God has revealed Himself in nature and in our consciences (Romans 1:18-22; 2:14-15). Hence, God has revealed truth to man apart from the Bible. For instance, a carpenter must learn his trade from information not found in the Bible. Still, the Bible teaches that everything Christians need to live godly and wholesome lives can be found in the Bible.

Therefore, the Bible is adequate to equip the believer for "every good work" (2 Timothy 3:16-17; 2 Peter 1:2-3). We may need extra-biblical information to lead a person to Christ, to learn a trade, or to keep up with current news. But, the Bible, by itself, is sufficient to lead a believer to live the victorious Christian life.

Physical ailments, including chemical imbalances in the brain, demand the attention of medical doctors; but the soul of a person needs only the Word of God and the power of the indwelling Holy Spirit. A person does not need Jesus plus Sigmund Freud to live a wholesome life. He needs Jesus alone. True biblical counseling is done from the Bible alone. God does not need Sigmund Freud. I do not deny that Freud may have occasionally stumbled onto truths despite his atheistic world view. However, if these truths will aid a person in living the Christian life, then they are already in the Bible. The church does not need to integrate the Bible and Freud; instead, we must test Freud with the Word and reject any of his teachings that contradict God's inerrant Word.

A brief sample of disagreements between the teachings of Scripture and that of modern psychology will expose the incompatibility that exists concerning the two systems of thought. The Bible views man as a willful sinner in need of God's redemption (Romans 3:10, 23; 6:23; Matthew 11:28), while modern psychology usually views its clients as victims in need of secular psychological wisdom. The Bible declares God's absolute moral laws (which man can only obey through Christ's power), but modern psychology often teaches moral relativism (each person may decide what is right for his or her self; there are no universal moral laws). The Bible calls destructive behavior habitual sin (Galatians 5:19-21), whereas modern psychology refers to it as an "addiction" or a "mental illness." The scriptures call man to repentance (Isaiah 45:22; Ephesians 4:27; Matthew 3:2; John 8:11), but psychology directs him to the wisdom of man for mental healing.

The Word of God tells us to focus on Christ, the problem-solver (Matthew 11:28; Colossians 2:8-10), but psychologists recommend that we focus on our problems in order to resolve them. God's infallible Word commands us to put God first, others second, and ourselves third (Matthew 6:33; Philippians 2:3-4; Mark 12:30-31), whereas psychology instructs us to put ourselves first. The Bible commands us to pursue a life of self-denial (Mark 8:34); however, psychologists encourage us to seek higher self-esteem. The written Word of God states that one of man's most basic problems is that he loves himself too much (2 Timothy 3:2; Mark 10:35-45), while psychology coaches man to learn to love himself more.

The Bible states that believers are no longer slaves to sin; we are now slaves to righteousness (Romans 6:17-18; 1 Corinthians 10:13). However, modern psychologists believe that even their Christian clients are slaves to hurts from their past and slaves to unconscious wounds. Finally, the scriptures teach the believer to focus on the future (the return of Christ) and to leave the past behind (Titus 2:12-13;

Philippians 3:13-14; 4:4-9, 13), while modern psychologists teach their clients to focus on their past hurts.

I do not pretend that all secular psychologists (and Christians who utilize secular psychological principles) adhere to every one of the above modern psychological principles. However, the honest student of modern psychological theory will have to admit that the principles listed above are common themes currently being utilized in counseling by Christians and non-Christians alike.

As Christians, God has called us to renew our minds with His Word. We should not conform to the world and its beliefs (Romans 12:1-2). We must reject the wisdom of man when it contradicts the Word of God (1 Thessalonians 5:21-22; James 3:13-18).

God wants us to meditate on principles from His Word, rather than follow the counsel of the wicked (Psalm 1:1-3), for when the blind lead the blind, both fall into a ditch (Luke 6:39). We are not to fellowship with darkness (2 Corinthians 6:14-18); we are to walk in the light of Christ and His Word (John 8:12). When we do so, the Holy Spirit will bear His fruit in our lives: "love, joy, peace, patience, kindness, goodness, faithfulness, gentleness, and self-control" (Galatians 5:22-23). The peace that Jesus gives us is a peace that the world cannot give or even understand (John 14:27; Philippians 4:7). Therefore, we must reject this counterfeit peace which the world offers. For the wisdom of the world will always view the cross of Christ as foolishness; yet, apart from the cross of Christ there is no genuine, lasting peace and abundant life (1 Corinthians 1:18-25; 2 Corinthians 2:6-16; John 10:10). As true followers of the Lord Jesus Christ, it is time to destroy our idols, for "if the Son shall make you free, you shall be free indeed" (John 8:36).

CHAPTER 29

RESCUING THE BIBLE FROM BISHOP SPONG

by Phil Fernandes

Since John Shelby Spong is the Episcopal bishop of Newark, New Jersey, the question immediately arises, "Can anything good come out of Newark?" Personally, I hope this question can be answered in the affirmative (for I was born in Newark). Still, the teachings of Bishop Spong cannot be viewed, from a conservative evangelical perspective, as good and wholesome spiritual guidance.

His best selling book *Rescuing the Bible From Fundamentalism* is filled with liberal theological speculation void of any basis in fact. In this book, he pleads with his readers to reject a literal interpretation of Scripture so that modern "thinking" people will be attracted to this updated form of Christianity (p. 233-237). However, one can only find truth in Spong's book if one interprets his work in the same fashion that Spong interprets the Bible. For Spong's work is clearly not literally true.

Contradictions abound in Spong's book. He repeatedly passes judgment on conservative evangelicals for passing judgment on others (p. 4-8). But, if it is wrong for evangelicals to judge others, then what right does Spong have when he condemns the views of evangelicals? If Spong rejects moral absolutes, can he consistently denounce as wrong the moral judgments made by those who literally interpret the Bible?

Spong cries "foul" when orthodox Christians condemn the practices of homosexuality and premarital sex (p. 7-8). He considers the Bible to have been written by "prescientific" and "prejudiced" men living in a "sexist society" (p. 15, 25-26) According to Spong, their biases against women and homosexuals cannot be accepted by modern man. Spong never addresses the detrimental public health consequences of homosexuality and promiscuity. He never entertains the possibility that the Bible is right and the modern view of morality is wrong. Apparantly, he assumes the "modern" view is correct merely because it is newer than the "traditional" view. He never argues for this unwarranted assumption.

It appears that Spong's god and ultimate authority is modern culture. Instead of judging modern culture by the truths found in the Bible, Spong assumes the truth of modern culture and then passes judgment on the Bible (p. 16). In short, Bishop Spong worships at the altar of political correctness. He fails to realize that there is no such thing as a politically correct martyr. If the authors of Scripture were committed to accepting whatever their culture thought was sacred, then they would not have been persecuted. Paul did not seek favor from men (Galatians 1:10). Unfortunately, this cannot be said of Bishop Spong.

Due to his acceptance of modern cultural views and the evolutionary model, Spong rejects the inspiration and inerrancy of the Bible, the deity and virgin birth of Christ, and the doctrine of the Trinity. He also rejects the Fall of man as a historical event, deplores the idea that salvation comes only through Christ, and finds the bodily resurrection of Christ to be unworthy of belief (p. 232-236).

Spong ignores his own modern cultural zeal while assuming that the ancient cultural zeal of the biblical authors prejudiced their writings (p. 15). Spong states that "miracle and magic" were a part of the world in which the biblical authors lived (p.153); however, he never mentions that antisupernaturalism (a bias against the possibility of miracles) and skepticism are a part of the world in which he lives. If the apostles could have been biased by their culture, could not Bishop Spong suffer from the prejudices of his own culture? Spong does not realize the extent that his mind has been shaped by modern culture. Instead, he repeatedly charges the biblical authors with ignorance (p. 25), and assumes that modern man is "in the know."

Spong admits that Christ's deity was established as dogma in the church as early as 80AD (p.149), yet he never explains how a legend could develop while eyewitnesses who knew Christ were still alive and leading the church. (Actually, ancient creeds found in the New Testament—Philippians 2:5-11; Romans 10:9; 1 Timothy 3:16; John 1:1-5—teach the deity of Christ and are dated several decades earlier than 80AD. Also, Paul clearly taught the deity of Christ and his writings all date before 67AD.) Spong never addresses the issue of how the apostles could be willing to die for mere fairy tales (Christ's deity and bodily resurrection).

Instead of interpreting the Bible in its natural sense, Bishop Spong psychoanalyzes Paul and concludes that Paul was a frustrated homosexual who refused to live out his passions (p. 116-127). This exercise in highly creative spec-ulation illustrates how far off track a person could go if he or she refuses to interpret the Bible literally. Apparantly,

Spong doesn't think we can trust the first generation church to accurately tell us what they witnessed concerning Christ's life, but he expects us to accept his psychological diagnosis of a person (the apostle Paul) who has been dead for nearly 2,000 years. And, to make matters worse, Spong isn't even a psychologist! One senses a double standard and a large dosage of intellectual snobbery in Spong's ramblings.

Although Spong refers to the Bible as "our treasured book," he believes that its authors were scientifically ignorant. Much of this negative assessment is probably based on his naive acceptance of the evolution model (p. 38-39). Still, he accuses the authors of Scripture of teaching that the earth is flat and that the sun revolves around the earth (p. 26). He also asserts that the Bible promotes slavery, stealing, and the murdering of innocent people (p. 17-19). If Spong is right in his interpretation of the Bible on these points, then why should we take his advice and reinterpret the Bible in a symbolic way? Why not simply trash this error-laden book and be done with it? Why treasure a fallible book with so many errors? Of course, one could conclude (as I do) that Spong has in fact misinterpreted the Bible in these areas.

Spong acts as if the speculation of liberal scholars has produced infallible and unquestionable conclusions (p. 10). Anyone who accepts the inspiration, inerrancy, and reliability of the Bible is accused by Bishop Spong of anti-intellectualism (p. 9). Apparently, Spong has never heard of conservative evangelical Bible scholars such as F. F. Bruce, Gleason Archer Jr., Bruce Metzger, and Merrill Unger. Though Spong deplores the idea of an infallible Bible, he accepts modern liberal criticism of the Bible without question. It seems that he has granted infallibility to modern cultural views.

Spong redefines Christian love as a tolerance for lifestyles that the Bible unambiguously condemns as sinful (p. 4). Due to his denial of a historical Fall of man, Spong fails to see that we humans are not experts when it comes to love. Due to our depravity, we are experts only when sin is concerned. If we wish to discover how love would respond to a given situation or lifestyle, we must turn to the God of the Bible. For God is love, and He has revealed Himself in His Word.

Bishop Spong refuses to worship the God of the literal Bible (p. 24). He believes we need a changing Christianity, a Christianity that evolves in order to be acceptable to each new generation (p. 230). But, the early Christians were willing to die for their faith rather than compromise biblical truth due to societal pressures. The Christianity that Spong proposes is not worthy of the name "Christianity." It is the antithesis of historic and biblical Christianity.

If we rescue the Bible from Bishop Spong and allow it to speak authoritatively, then the Book of Proverbs warns us not to go the way of Spong. For the Word of God states, "Trust in the Lord with all your heart, and do not lean on your own understanding. In all your ways acknowledge Him, and He will make your paths straight. Do not be wise in your own eyes; fear the Lord and turn away from evil" (Proverbs 3:5-7).

The reader must not "hesitate between two positions" (1 Kings 18:21). You may trust in an inerrant Bible, or go the way of Bishop Spong. "But as for me and my house, we will serve the Lord" (Joshua 24:15).

CHAPTER 30

THE CHRISTIAN, THE SECOND AMENDMENT, AND SELF-DEFENSE

by: Eric S. Purcell

FOREWORD

And He said to them, 'But now, whoever has a money bag is to take it along, likewise also a bag, and whoever has no sword is to sell his coat and buy one.' They said, 'Lord, look, here are two swords.' And He said to them, 'It is enough.'

—*Luke 22:36, 38*

A well regulated militia, being necessary to the security of a free state, the right of the people to keep and bear arms, shall not be infringed.

—*The 2nd Amendment to the*
United States Constitution

INTRODUCTION

There are two questions that need to be addressed in this chapter:

(1) Does the 2nd Amendment to the United States Constitution guarantee an individual right to bearing arms for self-defense?

(2) I am a believer; I have accepted Jesus as my Savior and Lord; can I or should I bear arms for self-defense?

To condense these questions even more, our basic goal in this chapter is to discover whether or not we can, by law, bear arms in self-defense and whether or not we can, by Scripture, bear arms in self-defense. It must also be stated that even if we are guaranteed the right to keep and bear arms by law it does not necessarily mean that we are required to do so. The choice to exercise a right is a matter of personal application, an appeal to the conscience. My arguments in this chapter are not an attempt to persuade a Christian that it is an obligation, either by law or by Scripture, to use arms.

THE CONSTITUTION AND THE 2ND AMENDMENT

The United States Constitution is not a divinely inspired document. It does not hold authority over the believer on the same level as Holy Scripture. Scripture is ". . . inspired by God and profitable for teaching, for reproof, for correction, for training in righteousness; so that the man of God may be adequate, equipped for every good work." (2 Timothy 3:16-17)[1] In accordance with the doctrine of *sola scriptura*, Scripture is the Christian's only authority for faith and practice. The Constitution is merely a man-made document that governs the institution of federal government, and that only here in the United States.

However, as the Constitution itself states, it is the "law of the land."[2] The purpose of the Constitution is to establish a system of federal government and to limit that system to a strict, closely defined role of responsibility and authority.[3] To reiterate this belief, the Constitution's 10th Amendment specifically states that, "The powers not delegated to the United States by the Constitution, nor prohibited by it to the states, are reserved to the states respectively, or to the people."[4]

Probably the most severe restriction upon the federal government is the guarantee of the individual's right to keep and bear arms as contained in the 2nd Amendment. This is the point where much modern debate is concerned. There is the belief that the 2nd Amendment does not guarantee individual rights but does guarantee the collective rights of a state-organized militia unit. This is the first false view of the 2nd Amendment that we shall discuss. In order to discuss this issue, one thing needs to be understood:

> On every question of construction [of the Constitution] let us carry ourselves back to the time when the Constitution was adopted, recollect the spirit manifested in the debates, and instead of trying what meaning may be squeezed out of the text, or invented against it, conform to the probable one in which it was passed.[5]

Mr. Jefferson's statement, above, is *the key* to an understanding of the 2nd Amendment. Those who oppose the traditional interpretation of the 2nd Amendment in an attempt to invent against it a supposedly "enlightened" interpretation trot out many political experts and many law scholars who give their opinion of what the founders meant. This work is not even going to deal with those arguments since they are, at best, specious. It is much more informative, historically accurate, and logically founded to look at the beliefs of the gentlemen who argued for the concepts of and wrote the text for the 2nd Amendment, or are at least contemporaries of those who did.

Does the 2nd Amendment guarantee an individual right or a collective right?

> The whole of the Bill [of Rights] is a declaration of the right of the people at large or considered as individuals ... It establishes some rights of the individual as unalienable and which consequently, no majority has a right to deprive them of.[6]

> And that the said Constitution be never construed to authorize Congress to infringe the just liberty of the Press, or the rights of Conscience; or to prevent the people of the United States, who are peaceable citizens, from keeping their own arms;...[7]

> The people are not to be disarmed of their weapons. They are left in full possession of them.[8]

> Last Monday a string of amendments were presented to the lower House; these altogether respected personal liberty ...[9]

> This [Second Amendment] may be considered as the true palladium of liberty .... The right of self defence is the first law of nature: in most governments it has been the study of rulers to confine this right within the narrowest limits possible.

Wherever standing armies are kept up, and the right of the people to keep and bear arms is, under any colour or pretext whatsoever, prohibited, liberty, if not already annihilated, is on the brink of destruction. In England, the people have been disarmed, generally, under the specious pretext of preserving the game: a never failing lure to bring over the landed aristocracy to support any measure, under that mask, though calculated for very different purposes. True it is, their bill of rights seems at first view to counteract this policy: but the right of bearing arms is confined to protestants, and the words suitable to their condition and degree, have been interpreted to authorise the prohibition of keeping a gun or other engine for the destruction of game, to any farmer, or inferior tradesman, or other person not qualified to kill game. So that not one man in five hundred can keep a gun in his house without being subject to a penalty.[10] [emphasis mine]

Little more can reasonably be aimed at, with respect to the people at large, than to have them properly armed and equipped;...[11]

No Free man shall ever be debarred the use of arms.[12]

The preceding is not an exhaustive investigation of the statements of the founding fathers and their contemporaries but it is a very representative sample of their thought. It should be intuitively obvious to even the most casual observer that the original intent of the 2nd Amendment was to guarantee the individual's right to keep and bear arms in self-defense.

Along these lines of discussion, for an opponent of the 2nd Amendment to assert that the guarantee of the right to keep and bear arms applies only to the authorized authorities that, in turn, protect the rights of citizens is also a false view. It has been stated that the present National Guard system has replaced the system of state militias and that, therefore, the right to keep and bear arms for the state militias applies only to the National Guard or to local or federal law enforcement agencies. There are several problems with this view. First, it has already been shown that intent of the 2nd Amendment was to guarantee the right of individual citizens. Second, it would have been anathema (to borrow a Scriptural term) for our founding fathers to assert that the protection of self (life, family, property, etc.) was to be surrendered entirely to a tool of federal government, which the National Guard is when called into federal service. It would also have been unthinkable for our founding fathers to make the requirement that the right of self-defense be surrendered entirely to local law enforcement agencies. Recent events such as the "sniper" murders in Washington, D.C., prove beyond a shadow of a doubt that local law enforcement, at its most alert and well equipped, cannot guarantee the safety of every citizen at all times. As a matter of fact even an armed citizen cannot guarantee his or her own safety at all times but at least has a fighting chance if required to protect life and limb from the evildoer. To say that the right to keep and bear arms applies only to agencies authorized by Congress would, to our founding fathers, be the same as placing the security of the henhouse in the sole possession of the foxes.

The US Ninth Circuit Court of Appeals published its opinion on the 2nd Amendment recently. Their interpretation of the issue is that the amendment does not guarantee individual rights but rights as a collective and that collective only exists as is legally authorized by a state in order to form a military unit (the militia). The opinion sites a plethora of case law (both federal and state) and also explores the semantics of the 2nd Amendment. Missing from their analysis of the meaning of the 2nd Amendment are the items listed earlier in this chapter. No attempt was made to determine the meaning of the amendment by researching the documents produced by the authors of the amendment or their contemporaries. The sited case law is, in my opinion, irrelevant since most of the case law sited also does not take into consideration the evidence here provided for the interpretation of the amendment. The first source sited as supporting the court's opinion has been proven to be fraudulent and has even led to the resignation of the author's university teaching position.[13] Still, the court sited this work in their opinion and blatantly ignored the preponderance of evidence that the 2nd Amendment guarantees the unalienable individual right to keep and bear arms.

The second false interpretation of the 2nd Amendment is that it merely applies to persons keeping arms for hunting or sporting purposes. A brief historical investigation reveals that the 2nd Amendment was written immediately following a war for the independence of the colonies in America. That war was fought because of the oppression of government over a free populace. It must also be understood that the war was fought, primarily, by armed citizens, the state militias (citizen soldiers), and not by an organized federal army. An organized army was raised by the Continental Congress, an army known as the Continental Army, but even so individual citizens reported for duty, for the most part, armed with their own personal firearms and accessories. The point being made here is that the Congress was not concerned with protecting the rights of hunters and target shooters, they were concerned with protecting the freedoms of recently liberated citizens from the threats of foreign invasion and government tyranny.

There are several quotes that are especially useful in fortifying this line of reasoning:

> The right of the people to keep and bear arms has been recognized by the General Government; but the best security of that right after all is, the military spirit, that taste for martial exercises, which has always distinguished the free citizens of these States ... Such men form the best barrier to the liberties of America.[14]

> The constitutions of most of our States assert that all power is inherent in the people; that... it is their right and duty to be at all times armed;...[15]

> Before a standing army can rule, the people must be disarmed; as they are in almost every kingdom of Europe. The supreme power in America cannot enforce unjust laws by the sword; because the whole body of the people are armed, and constitute a force superior to any bands of regular troops...[16] [emphasis mine]

> To disarm the people [is] the best and most effectual way to enslave them ...[17]

> to preserve liberty it is essential that the whole body of the people always possess arms, and be taught alike, especially when young, how to use them ...[18]

> Besides the advantage of being armed, which the Americans possess over the people of almost every other nation,... in the several kingdoms of Europe,... the governments are afraid to trust the

people with arms.[19]

The importance of this article [Second Amendment] will scarcely be doubted by any persons, who have duly reflected upon the subject. The militia is the natural defence of a free country against sudden foreign invasions, domestic insurrections, and *domestic usurpations of power by rulers*.[20] [emphasis mine]

Guard with jealous attention the public liberty. Suspect every one who approaches that jewel. Unfortunately, nothing will preserve it but down-right force. Whenever you give up that force, you are ruined.[21]

God forbid we should ever be 20 years without such a rebellion. The people cannot be all, & always, well informed... *what country can preserve it's liberties if their rulers are not warned from time to time that their people preserve the spirit of resistance?* Let them take arms... The tree of liberty must be refreshed from time to time with the blood of patriots & tyrants. It is it's natural manure.[22] [emphasis mine]

All of the preceding quotes from the founding fathers and their contemporaries are a matter of public record and can be found in myriad publications and websites that are concerned with the RKBA (right to keep and bear arms) issue.[23] The fact that they are well known and heavily used does not affect their truthfulness. The fact that they are ignored or misinterpreted by the opponents of the 2nd Amendment also does not affect their truthfulness. The historical record stands: the 2nd Amendment guarantees the individual right of ownership and possession of arms for the matter of self-defense.[24]

Having established the preceding facts, one more issue needs to be dealt with. That issue is the source of human rights; are human rights granted by government or merely protected by government and granted from some more supreme authority? In order to correctly interpret and apply the Constitution, one must also include an understanding of the foundational principles that led to the authoring of the Declaration of Independence.

The Declaration of Independence was written because government was ignoring and violating the basic rights of humans, individually and collectively. One need merely look at the list of grievances against the Crown as contained in the Declaration in order to see that the colonists were outraged that fundamental rights had been violated and that they had petitioned the Crown on many occasions in order to restore the rule of law and the recognition of unalienable human rights. It was the contention of the authors of the Declaration that rights are granted by the Creator (God), protected by human government, and are therefore unalienable. This means that rights cannot be granted by human government and can only be revoked in accordance with the rule of law (for violations of the law such as murder where the right to life and liberty is forfeit). This is the foundational concept for the Bill of Rights, the first ten Amendments to the Constitution. These Amendments are a written recognition of unalienable human rights that the newly formed federal government must acknowledge and protect. The 2nd Amendment does not *grant* US citizens the right to keep and bear arms, it merely *acknowledges* and *guarantees* that right as previously existing and untouchable.

THE SCRIPTURES

Having established that the 2nd Amendment guarantees

the individual, unalienable right to keep and bear arms for self-defense, we as Christians must now examine the Scriptures to determine their input on the matter. It cannot be stated too strongly that our views, whether they be political or social or religious, must be formulated in light of and founded solely upon Scripture. Just because human government protects a right or grants a privilege does not mean that Christians are necessarily obligated or free to exercise that right or privilege. For example, it is legal in the United States to abort an unborn child. Scripture clearly teaches that such an act is murder and an abomination before the Lord. Another example is that in the United States it is acceptable and even encouraged to lead a homosexual lifestyle. Once again Scripture clearly teaches that homosexuality is an aberration and an abomination before the Lord. In short, just because we can do something by human law does not mean that we can do that thing by Scripture.

There are two Scriptural issues that must be investigated. I will list them here for clarity.

1. Does Scripture prohibit self-defense?
2. Did Jesus teach that resistance to the evildoer, in all cases, is wrong?

These two simple questions must be answered in order to understand the fundamental Scriptural teaching concerning self-defense. The key issue here is not the right to bear arms, it is the Scriptural teaching on self-defense that, naturally, would weigh heavily on a Christian's decision to keep and bear arms for the purposes of self-defense.

There are several portions of scripture that deal with self-defense. The first we shall examine is the teachings of the Lord Jesus Himself. During the celebration of the Passover meal immediately prior to Jesus' arrest, trials, and crucifixion, Jesus dealt with this issue with His twelve apostles. In the Gospel of Luke 22:36 and 38, we are told the following:

> And He said to them, 'But now, whoever has a money bag is to take it along, likewise also a bag, and whoever has no sword is to sell his coat and buy one.' They said, 'Lord, look, here are two swords.' And He said to them, 'It is enough.

Jesus, being fully-God and fully-human, understood the perverse sinfulness of human nature better than any other man who has ever lived. He would, very soon after these events, be sending His messengers into a hostile world to travel great distances to proclaim His message of redemption. This hostile world would be filled with all sorts of danger (from dangerous beasts to even more dangerous evil men). While it is true that the Christian's reliance should be solely upon God for protection and guidance, Jesus did instruct His Apostles to purchase swords. In the 1st century AD the sword was the "weapon of choice" by civilians and military alike for offense and self-defense. The sword was the "assault weapon" of the world until the separate inventions of gunpowder and the firearm. It is extremely interesting that the Lord Himself would instruct His apostles, men who would shortly be concerned with the overwhelming priority of proclaiming the Gospel to a lost world, to procure weapons and to take provisions along with them on their journeys.

It is also interesting to note that for a group of twelve men (one of whom would soon be dead after completing his role as the betrayer of the Messiah), Jesus said that two swords would be sufficient. Not everyone is called or equipped to use arms for self-defense. It has never been the argument of the author that everyone should carry a firearm "just because they can." See the afterword of this chapter for a more thorough discussion of this matter.

The second portion of Scripture we should look to is contained in the book of Nehemiah. Nehemiah had received permission from King Artaxerxes (who had the Jews in captivity at that time) to return to Jerusalem and rebuild the city that had lain in ruins for a very long time.[25] Nehemiah returned to Jerusalem and was surrounded on all sides by enemies who wished to not only ridicule the work of the Jews but also wanted to kill them to prevent the re-establishment of a Jewish capital city. Nehemiah's first priority was to rebuild the wall surrounding the city. This work was completed in fifty-two days. This amazing feat was accomplished even though an extra burden was placed upon the workers engaged in this project.

> Our enemies said, 'They will not know or see until we come among them, kill them and put a stop to the work.' When the Jews who lived near them came and told us ten times, 'They will come up against us from every place where you turn,' then I stationed men in the lowest parts of the space behind the wall, the exposed places, and I stationed the people in families with their swords, spears and bows. When I saw their fear, I rose and spoke to the nobles, the officials and the rest of the people: 'Do not be afraid of them; remember the Lord who is great and awesome, and fight for your brothers, your sons, your daughters, your wives and your houses.' When our enemies heard that we knew it, and that God had frustrated their plan, then all of us returned to the wall, each one to his work. From that day on, half of my servants carried on the work while half of them held the spears, the shields, the bows and the breastplates; and the captains were behind the whole house of

Judah. Those who were rebuilding the wall and those who carried burdens took their load with one hand doing the work and the other holding a weapon. As for the builders, each wore his sword girded at his side as he built, while the trumpeter stood near me. I said to the nobles, the officials and the rest of the people, 'the work is great and extensive, and we are separated on the wall far from one another. At whatever place you hear the sound of the trumpet, rally to us there. Our God will fight for us." So we carried on the work with half of them holding spears from dawn until the stars appeared. At that time I also said to the people, 'Let each man with his servant spend the night within Jerusalem so that they may be a guard for us by night and a laborer by day.' So neither I, my brothers, my servants, nor the men of the guard who followed me, none of us removed our clothes, each took his weapon even to the water.[26]

It is interesting to note that Nehemiah's faith was that *God would fight for them.* Yet he still required that his workers arm themselves while working, while resting, and even while going to get water for refreshment. He provided for the defense of the weakest points of the city walls and always had the trumpeter with him so that he could sound the alarm at a moment's notice. Nehemiah was most assuredly aware of the Exodus of Israel from Egypt under the leadership of Moses and the conquest of the Promised Land by Joshua and the Israelites. He knew that God had promised the land to them and that he would remove the pagan nations from before them. However, Nehemiah also knew that God used the physical effort of the armies of Israel, and the military genius of Joshua (and Moses before him), to accomplish His will in protecting Israel and in securing the Promised Land for themselves. It is entirely possible for God to miraculously intervene and destroy the enemies of His people; see Exodus Chapter 14 where God miraculously destroys the armies of Egypt as they pursue Israel across the parted Red Sea. However, it is a more common event in Scripture for God to raise up a person (Samson, Gideon, and King David, for example) who individually or as the leader of the armies of God's people brings victory against their enemies. The point being made here is that more often than not in Scripture, God provides for the physical self-defense and physical victories of His people, over those who would do them harm, through the actions of Godly men and women and that sometimes those actions require the resorting to the bearing of arms of war. It is also interesting to note from the passages quoted from Nehemiah that the people were instructed to "fight for your brothers, your sons, your daughters, your wives and your houses." The priority here was to protect family and property from those who seek to destroy them. It is helpful to compare this statement to the statement of Jesus when he said, "But I say to you, do not resist an evil person; but whoever slaps you on your right cheek, turn the other to him also. If anyone wants to sue you and take your shirt, let him have your coat also. Whoever forces you to go one mile, go with him two."[27] The key to understanding Jesus' words and Nehemiah's instructions is the level of force being directed at the innocent person. The stated goal of Nehemiah's enemies was to kill the Jews. None of the offenses listed by Jesus are life threatening. There is a vast difference between a slap in the face and being confronted by an evil person who possesses the means to kill you. Another key to understanding Jesus' words is that all the actions listed by Jesus are directed at you or I as individuals. He did not discuss, in these passages, a threat to our children, our spouses, or our friends and other family members. The choice to not defend myself against an evil person is my choice to make and is a matter of conscience. If my spouse or my child was in imminent physical danger then I would think that I have the moral obligation to protect them by whatever means are necessary to eliminate that threat – which does not necessarily require the use of lethal force but may involve such measures.

CONCLUSION

It has been shown that the Constitution of the United States protects the right of the individual to keep and bear arms for self-defense. It has been shown that the concept of self-defense includes protection from the evildoer as an individual or the evildoer in the broader sense of government refusing to acknowledge the fundamental rights of the people. It has been shown that Scripture allows for the exercise of the right of self-defense. The only question that remains is the one that must be answered by each and every individual believer. "Will I exercise the right of self-defense by keeping and bearing arms for the protection of my life, my family's life, and the life of others that I may have to protect?"

I cannot answer that question for you. That is between you and God. I would humbly suggest that this question be given attention in prayer, study of the Word, and Christian meditation upon Godly principles. God's will for you, wherever it may lead you, is the goal of your life. Don't allow preconceived ideas, fears, or desires to determine what God's will is for you. Allow the Holy Spirit to speak to you and guide you through Scripture, through your Church fellowship, and through the events of your life as interpreted by God's Word. May the grace of the Lord Jesus be with you now and forever and may His will be done in all things and our lives be for His glory alone.

AFTERWORD

While I believe that it is every human's right to keep and bear arms for self-defense, I do not believe that every human should do so. This may sound elitist but I do not believe that all humans possess the sense of responsibility, the intelligence, or the moral guideposts necessary to correctly exercise the right to keep and bear arms.

Firearms are used to destroy things. While it is not true, as Hollywood portrays, that shooting someone with a pistol or even a rifle will pick that person up and throw them backwards twenty-feet through a brick wall, firearms are designed to inflict damage upon their intended target. Punching holes in a piece of paper at the shooting range is one thing and some firearms are designed to do just that. However, the vast majority of firearms are intended to deliver a bullet to a destination (usually living flesh), with a very high degree of accuracy, and inflict as much destruction as possible. The possession of such a tool provides the possessor with an awesome power.

Along with this awesome power comes awesome responsibility, a need for a certain level of competence, and the need for a moral guidepost. It would be unthinkable for me to point my firearm at another human being unless another innocent human life (including my own) was in danger. It would be unthinkable for me to use my firearm to threaten another innocent human being. As a matter of fact, when confronted with a situation that may turn deadly, my first option is to get away from that situation as quickly as possible – sometimes this option cannot be exercised but that doesn't remove it from the list of viable alternatives to the use of deadly force. Anyone who uses a firearm for self-defense should be very senstive to what are called the "shoot, don't shoot"[28] scenarios. The decision to utilize deadly force should never be taken lightly and only as a last resort. My father instructed me in the basic responsibilities of firearms ownership at a very young age. He was also responsible for a large portion of my competence in the subject. The moral guidepost that I possess comes from Scripture and my personal relationship with the Lord Jesus. Human life is sacred and I shall not seek to destroy it. I never seek out dangerous situations so that I may play the "gunslinger" and attempt to save the day. As far as it is possible for me, I attempt to remain at peace with all men.[29] Some people are just not equipped to keep and bear arms in a sensible, responsible, moral way. I would actively encourage these people to *not* exercise the right to keep and bear arms because the usual outcome of their choice to do so is detrimental to those of us who do exercise responsibility, morality, and common-sense (best case) and may also result in the death of an innocent person (worst case).

I trust that the Lord Jesus will protect me and my family and that He will lead us in His will. However, I still take the necessary steps to be prepared to defend the innocent from the evildoer. As stated in the conclusion to this chapter, that is a choice that each and every one of us must make individually.

ENDNOTES

[1] Unless otherwise indicated, Scripture taken from the NEW AMERICAN STANDARD BIBLE®, Copyright © 1960, 1962, 1963, 1968, 1971, 1972, 1973, 1975, 1977, 1995 by the Lockman Foundation. Used by permission.

[2] United States Constitution, Article VI, Clause 2.

[3] See the United States Constitution, Article I, Section 8, Clause 1 through Clause 18, inclusive.

[4] United States Constitution, 10th Amendment.

[5] Thomas Jefferson, letter to Justice William Johnson, June 12, 1823.

[6] Albert Gallatin of the New York Historical Society, October 7, 1789.

[7] Samuel Adams, Debates & Proceedings in the Convention of the Commonwealth of Massachusetts, 86-87 (February 6, 1788).

[8] Zachariah Johnson, 3 Elliot, Debates at 646 (June 25, 1788).

[9] Senator William Grayson of Virginia in a letter to Patrick Henry, June 12, 1789.

[10] Saint George Tucker, *Blackstone's Commentaries* (1803), Volume 1, Appendix, Note D.

[11] Alexander Hamilton, The Federalist Papers # 29.

[12] Thomas Jefferson, Proposed Virginia Constitution.

[13] The source discussed here is *Arming America: The Origins of a National Gun Culture* by Michael Bellesiles, formerly of Emory University. A committee made up of scholars from Princeton University, Harvard University and the University of Chicago investigated Mr. Bellesiles' work. They determined that the evidence presented in the book showed "evidence of falsification," "egregious misrepresentation," and "exaggeration of data," and stated that "his scholarly integrity is seriously in question." Emory University prompted the investigation and announced shortly thereafter that Mr. Bellesiles had resigned and stated that he was "guilty of unprofessional and misleading work." The committee went on to state that, "Every aspect of his work in the probate records [a source of the research] is deeply flawed," and that Mr. Bellesiles "appears not to have been systematic in selecting repositories or collections of probate records for examination, and his recording methods were at best primitive and altogether unsystematic."

[14] Gazette of the United States, October 14, 1789

[15] Thomas Jefferson letter to Justice John Cartwright, June 5, 1824. 1824.

[16] Noah Webster, "An Examination into the Leading Principles of the Federal Constitution", (1787).

[17] George Mason, 3 Elliot, Debates at 380 (June 14, 1788).

[18] Richard Henry Lee writing in Letters from the Federal Farmer to the Republic, Letter 18, January 25, 1788.

[19] James Madison, The Federalist Papers # 46.

[20] Joseph Story, *Commentaries on the Constitution of the United States* (1833), Book III at 746, § 1858.

[21] Patrick Henry, (Virginia Convention, June 5, 1788).

[22] Thomas Jefferson to William S. Smith on Nov. 13, 1787. *The Papers of Thomas Jefferson*, ed. Julian P. Boyd, vol. 12, p. 356 (1955).

[23] I am indebted to the several websites for the quotes used in this work. Among these are The Second Amendment Foundation (www.saf.org) and Gun Owners of America (www.gunowners.org).

[24] "Self-defense" refers not only to the protection of life, family, and private property but also to protection from illegitimate government.

[25] See Nehemiah chapters 1 and 2.

[26] Nehemiah 4:11-23.

[27] Matthew 5:39-41.

[28] Shoot/Don't-Shoot scenarios are those situations which law enforcement officers and self-defense-minded private citizens usually train for in order to prevent injuring or killing innocent persons and/or to prevent the use of excessive force. For example: a man with a knife in his hand jumps out from behind a tree about 75 feet away from an armed citizen. This is a "no shoot" situation due to the distances involved and the possibility that escalation of the incident may not be necessary (maybe you can get away, maybe he doesn't see you, etc.). However, if that man with a knife runs towards you, yelling that he intends to kill you, and you have no avenue of escape, the "no shoot" situation has suddenly become a situation where "shoot" is a viable option . . . deadly force has become necessary to protect innocent human life. All gun owners should think of these issues in a very serious manner.

[29] Romans 12:18.

CHAPTER 31

THREE CHEERS FOR THE TWO-PARTY SYSTEM

by Kurt Rinear

As Christians our primary duty is to seek the Lord's will and live lives that are pleasing to him. As Americans we have a duty to be informed and involved in our political process. In many ways the same trend we see in the spiritual life of the church — increasing abandonment of the traditional Christian faith, is also evident in the politics of our nation — increasing abandonment of conservative, Constitutional principles.

It comes as no surprise that the Democratic Party has been the sword-bearer for the liberal cause for decades. Supporting gun control, eco-extremism, abortion, welfare and a plethora of other left-wing social and economic agendas, the Democratic Party has been responsible for moving the United States closer and closer to socialism.

On the other side of the issue was the Republican Party,

the champion of the conservative cause, calling for a return to our Constitutional framework of limited government and individual responsibility. Yet most people in our time seem to be totally disillusioned by the political process, Christian and non-Christian alike. It seems as though no matter whom we vote for the size and power of government continue to grow. To most people something is terribly wrong with our political establishment but they can't seem to put their finger on it. And so, in response, most people, Christians included, take the "hands-off" attitude. It usually goes something like, "Well, my vote doesn't count. I can't make a difference. They're all crooks anyway." Christians, in particular, have retreated because they have worked so hard to get politicians elected who profess conservative, traditional values during the election, but then don't live up to their words once in office. Why is this happening? It can be summed up in one word: neo-conservatism. Adherents to this political philosophy are often referred to as *neo-cons*.

LEFT VS. RIGHT?

While most can agree that the Democratic Party has been the champion of liberal causes, what most of us are not aware of is that a subtle change has occurred in the political fabric of the right wing; a subtle change in ideology. To understand this change we need to look at political history.

In the 1960's the left-wing of American politics became more hard-edged, adopting many pro-communist stances. The right-wing, opposed to the spread of Communism, fought this new left. However, many in the left-wing were not happy with the rise of the pro-communist, anti-American faction. They disagreed with the revolutionary ideas that were coming out in the late 60's and were also displeased with the negative aspects of the social sex and drug culture. These individuals came to be known as neo-conservatives because their ideas were distinct from the hard line New Left and the Old Right.

Many in the Old Right began to see neo-conservatives as allies against the Left since the neo-conservatives were speaking out against many of the things the Right was. Because of this, neo-conservatives were welcomed into conservative circles. This acceptance became a fatal mistake for the true conservative Right. Over time many neo-conservative concepts began gaining mainstream acceptance in the Right and therefore in the political party of the Right, the Republican Party.

The problem with neo-conservatism is that, while opposed to many of the ideals of the extreme left, there was still an acceptance of many liberal presuppositions and beliefs. While neo-conservatives derided "liberal dogma" and the New Left, they still believed in big government and the welfare state that had been created by previous liberal leaders and were outspoken advocates of the Roosevelt Administration's New Deal. The neo-conservative concept of democracy is actually democratic socialism. They believe it is the purpose of government to be a cure of social ills. This radical difference in belief between neo-conservatives and members of the Old Right, also known as paleo-conservatives, began to bring the two groups at odds. As neo-conservative beliefs became more accepted in the mainstream of Republican thought, from the national level to the state and the local levels, in a top-down fashion, paleo-conservatives began to be pushed to the back of the party more and more. Many prominent neo-conservatives came to control major sources of conservative funding and began to choke off funds to Old right conservative organizations and think tanks, in an effort to control the positions of what was rapidly becoming the New Right.

WHAT'S SO WRONG WITH THE NEW RIGHT?

Nowhere can the differences between Old Right conservatives and neo-conservatives be seen more clearly than in the election landscape. In the 1996 Presidential race, the paleo-conservative Republican candidate, Pat Buchanan, was attacked with a ferocity rarely seen. Buchanan was hammered mercilessly by the liberal media establishment, but surprisingly enough, the most vitriolic attacks came from the members of his own party. His fellow Republicans labeled Buchanan as a fascist, racist, anti-Semite bigot. In the primary he was lambasted repeatedly by the neo-conservative Republican establishment in an attempt to discredit him and prop up the neo-conservative candidate, Bob Dole. All these attacks came from the party that prides itself on Reagan's 11th commandment: Speak no ill of your fellow Republican.

To understand the rational behind the attacks, and in so doing the current war in the Republican Party, it is essential to understand the different views of government. The paleo-conservative view is the view of our Founding Fathers. It is the belief that all rights are bestowed by God and that governments are instituted among men to protect those inalienable rights. The institution of that government is based upon the framework of Law. The government is constituted by the consent of the people. The powers that the people vest in the government are enumerated in the U.S Constitution and in the Constitutions of the respective states. One of the sad things about the average Christian's ignorance of politics and government is the misunderstanding of this point. We are a nation of laws and not men. The Apostle Paul directs us to be in subjection to the governing authorities in Romans chapter 13. He states that all authority comes from God, which our Founding Fathers recognized. The question we need to ask ourselves is what constitutes the governing authorities in America? Is it the President? Is it the Supreme Court or the Congress? Or are they simply ministers and instruments of the true governing authority, the authority of the people embodied in the Constitution?

The people, under law, are the true governing authority, not the arbitrary will of men in power. American founding father Thomas Paine summed up this concept as follows:

> A constitution is not the act of a government, but of a people constituting a government; and government without a constitution is power without a right. All power exercised over a nation, must have some beginning. It must be either delegated, or assumed. There are not other sources. All delegated power is trust, and all assumed power is usurpation. Time does not alter the nature and quality of either.

This concept of constituted power is the foundational principle of the Rule of Law. The law is a negative force used to punish the evildoer and protect the God given rights of the citizen. Because of sin there is a need for law that is superior to all individuals, including those who exercise political power. This is the only way to protect man from the ravages of criminals and the power of the state. Because fallen sinful men are the elected representatives, judges and executives of the State, the law must also prevent any one man's or group of men's lust for power to enable him to usurp the consented powers of the governed. This is accomplished in the separation of powers and checks and balances we see in our Constitution.

The problem with liberalism, which forms the core presuppositions and beliefs of neo-conservatism, is that it is based on a flawed view of man and sin. The liberal mindset is not new, it is millennia old. It can be traced back from Marx and Lenin to the Jacobins to the ancient Babylonians to a garden where man fell from grace under a lie that man would be as God. In the liberal mindset there is no God or man himself is god. As the German philosopher Nietzsche noted, if God is dead then all traditional values have died with him. There is no absolute standard of right and wrong. Man is left to himself to forge his own morality or exercise his will to power. This materialistic belief in power is at the core of the liberal assumption. Without God to guide man and organize society along principles of Biblical morality, man is left to create his own society and in so doing the State takes the place of God. Rights become not endowed by God but granted by the State.

While many neo-conservatives would consciously deny such a hard line leftist view, nevertheless, these underlying assumptions are the cause for the neo-conservative love affair with and absolute trust in big government.

A PARADIGM SHIFT

The net result of the neo-conservative control of the Republican Party is that the "conservative right" has moved to the left. This shift has left true, constitutional conservatives out in the cold and ineffectual in the party. Our country's political landscape has been a two-party system for the majority of our nation's existence. Only recently has there been a slew of third party options for voters to choose from. The reason for this is that many feel disenfranchised by the two major parties. Part of the problem, though, is public perception. The media continues to portray the two major parties as the only viable political parties available. This portrayal and acceptance by the public only serves to further entrench the power base of liberalism since both the Democratic Party and Republican Party share many of the same liberal ideologies. Both parties want to continue to move us towards ever expanding government. They simply disagree on the details of the expansion and the rate at which we are socialized.

It is important to note that not everyone in the Republican Party is neo-conservative. There are many fine conservatives who are fighting to return the Republican Party to the principles on which the nation was founded. However, just as many if not more have left the party believing that the only possible way to fight for true conservatism is outside the party. And many others have swallowed the neo-conservative mantra of "just give us more time." The real problem for those still fighting within the party is that the neo-conservative ideology is solidly fortified at the national and state levels and even at the local level in many counties. True conservatives are told to sacrifice their principles for the sake of building winning coalitions that just serve to further liberalize the party. As someone who was involved in Republican politics for many years, I got a firsthand taste of the struggle paleo-conservatives experience with the neo-conservatives. This struggle was not just ideological but also personal. I, like many others, was the recipient of ad-hominen attacks at times. This combination of factors has driven many solid conservatives from the Republican Party.

The traditional conservative view is being swept under the rug to make way for the New Right. It is called by many names. One of the most well known is the moniker "Compassionate Conservatism", which is just a pseudonym for a Republican-controlled, big government, welfare state. Yet the media portrays the neo-conservative right as the true right-wing. This has served to marginalize true conservative views. Anyone in the establishment who espouses constitutional principles is labeled an extremist and identified with fascism (which is actually left-wing, not right-wing), bigotry, hate mongering, etc. True conservatism is now the extreme fringe of the political right because the definition of "right-wing" has been usurped by the neo-conservatives. All we are left with is left-wing Democratic liberalism and right-wing Republican liberalism. Is it any surprise that so many are fed up with and disenfranchised by the political process?

THE POLITICS OF RELIGION

In order to solidify their power base in the Republican Party, the neo-conservative establishment has courted the religious right for years. This support is largely rhetoric and not substantive. Candidates frequently talk about family values and traditional morality yet their solutions are often more government intervention and more laws. The Republican leadership allows true conservatives to frame the platforms of the party and then usually turns around and ignores them. Unfortunately, the religious right, for the most part, has continued to take the bait. The neo-conservative leadership has actively courted the leaders of Christian conservative organizations. In 1994 the Republican leadership actually convinced Christian Coalition leader Ralph Reed to support removing the pro-life language from the party platform so as not to be "divisive" and to bring the party's platform more in line with the "public's view." Ralph Reed has since become a poster child for the neo-conservative influence in Christian politics. Despite the conservative views of the members of the Christian Coalition, that organization has been co-opted by the neo-cons through its national leadership, thereby moving the group to the left.

LESSER OF TWO EVILS

The response that many in the Republican Party have taken is to vote for the lesser of two evils. Conservatives are told that it is impossible to get a candidate elected who rates a nine or ten (ten being a true conservative one a one-to-ten scale), it's not politically viable. The Party must change things gradually. They claim that since the welfare state wasn't built overnight, taking decades to build, it stands to reason that it will take a long time to dismantle. In the meantime it is necessary to vote for a candidate who rates a four or a five, but at least it's better than voting for a one or two rated candidate by voting Democrat. But is it really? Voting for the lesser of two evils still promotes evil and entrenches that evil in power. It also prevents men who genuinely support the true conservative cause from ever being able to get into office and make a difference. And even if a handful do get in, they will not be powerful enough to stem the tide. This mentality prevents any real challenge to the established power base in government and the status quo is maintained. The size and scope of government continue to increase.

WHERE DO WE GO FROM HERE?

It is essential that Christians educate themselves on political issues and adopt a firm philosophy of government rooted in the eternal principles of the Word of God. Many Christians know their Bibles but know precious little about what the government is doing in their name or why they are doing it. As citizens of a free society, we have the obligation and responsibility to educate ourselves and be involved. As Thomas Jefferson stated:

> If a Nation expects to be ignorant and free in a state of civilization, it expects what never was and never will be... if we are to guard against ignorance and remain free, it is the responsibility of every American to be informed.

We need to vote for good candidates, not the lesser of two evils. The only way we can hold our elected representatives responsible is if we first become responsible. Our leaders are a microcosm of society as a whole. If we, the American people, will not govern ourselves then we will be governed by the iron fist of big government. If we do not understand the philosophy of neo-conservatism and recognize it for what it is, we will continue to see the foundation of our liberties erode before our eyes. It is my firm conviction that neo-conservatism is a far greater danger to liberty than any other form of liberalism. The reason is because it masquerades as conservatism. The reason it can do so is because most people are ignorant of it.

Many people think that our freedoms can never be taken away; that America will always be the Land of the Free and the Home of the Brave. The history of civilization does not bear this out. America is not special. There is no special dispensation from God guaranteeing that America will always be free. Over the last hundred years our liberty has eroded significantly. Many don't seem to realize it because it has been a gradual process — like the proverbial frog in the pot of boiling water.

It is time to take a stand for the principles that made this nation blessed by God. We need to fight in the political arena to secure the blessings of liberty for ourselves and our posterity but we need to fight with knowledge and understanding. We need to expose the truth about neo-conservatism and combat it if we are to return constitutional conservatism to its rightful place again.

CHAPTER 32

EPILOGUE: HOW SHOULD WE THEN LIVE?

In this book, the authors have discussed the biblical view of government and morality. We have argued that the leaders of Western civilization have rejected the God of the Bible, His moral laws, and His view of government. Hence, the world is heading down the deadly road to tyranny, a road which recognizes no limits to the growth of government and a road which does not check the power of sinful leaders. The question we must answer is this: *How should we then live?* If the movement towards a New World Order is really this far along, how should Christians respond? Is there anything we can do?

We believe that, as long as we have breath, good men and good women must stand up for that which is right and true. Though ultimately the future is in God's hands, we must join Him in His battle against evil. The authors believe that there are at least seven things Christians can do to combat the evil spirit of this age.

First, we must pray. We must pray for our nation, for the church (all true believers), and for the salvation of the lost. We cry out to God in prayer because we recognize our dependence on Him, the God who sits enthroned. Ultimately, the battle is a spiritual one (Ephesians 6:10-18) and, without God, there can be no victory. Even if the New World Order brings the Antichrist to power, the final victory belongs to our God and His people. For the day will come when our redeemer, the Lord Jesus, will take His stand upon the earth. He will defeat His enemies and wipe the tears from the eyes of His people—those who trust in Him alone for salvation.

Second, we must witness. Leading others to salvation in Jesus has always been and will always be the most powerful thing we can do. We cannot change cultures if we do not change hearts. We must tell others that we are sinners in desperate need of salvation, and that we cannot save ourselves (Romans 3:10, 23). We must proclaim the good news (i.e., the gospel) that God the Son became a man to die on the cross for our sins (John 1:1, 14; 3:16; 1 Peter 2:24; 3:18). He took our punishment for us and died as our substitute sacrifice (John 1:29). We must beseech others to trust in Jesus for salvation, for there is salvation in no other name (Acts 4:12; John 14:6; 11:25-26; 6:47). Once a person accepts Jesus as his only Savior, he is indwelt by the Holy Spirit (God the third Person of the Trinity). The Holy Spirit then begins to enlighten our minds to understand God's truth. Without the aid of the Holy Spirit, it is unlikely that we will be able to identify the evil workings of Lucifer, the spirit of the age, and we will be without God's power necessary to combat this evil.

Third, we must get informed. Before we can educate others, we must educate ourselves. We need to study God's Word and attend a Bible-believing, Bible-preaching church. Many churches today no longer preach the convicting, eternal truths of God's Word. Many churches today have compromised and surrendered to the spirit of this age, preaching self-ishness rather than self-denial. Many churches choose to proclaim a popular message that will increase attendance and funds, rather than a godly message that will increase godliness and combat evil. However, we need to know not only God's Word, but also God's world. We need to recognize the lies of Satan as well as the truths of God. We must be able to identify and expose the false, one-world religion (i.e., neo-paganism, worship of the earth) that opposes everything that is of God. We need to be knowledgeable about political issues as well. If we do not thoroughly understand the *Declaration of Independence, the United States Constitution,* and *the Bill of Rights,* we will not be able to identify and oppose the attempts to overthrow our government through unconstitutional and deceitful means. At the close of this chapter, the reader will be given a list of recommended books, organizations, and websites to help the reader get informed on the spiritual and political issues of our day.

Fourth, once we educate ourselves we must begin to educate others. Besides sharing our faith with others, we must teach others about the demonic and human conspiracy to enslave mankind through global government, and we must tell them how to combat this evil.

Fifth, we must vote wisely. We must study the views of the candidates and vote for those who defend the sovereignty of our country and the sanctity of human life. We must elect officials who take seriously their oath to the United States Constitution. We can no longer back and blindly trust one particular political party, expecting deliverance to come through neo-conservative and unconstitutional means. We need to face the reality that the leadership of both political parties is pro-UN, not pro-America. We must face the fact that we have lost the presidency to CFR-backed puppets who are hand-picked to further the goals of the New World Order. Instead of investing all our energy and time into the presidential race, we should focus our attention on the United States Congress, the only sliver of the federal government remaining where American citizens still have a say. We must reject the temptation to vote for the globalist of our choice.

Sixth, we must use our time wisely and not allow ourselves to get sidetracked. Spending all our time campaigning for one politician (even if he or she is a true constitutionalist) is not an effective use of one's time. Our free time should be devoted to spreading the gospel, educating others about the issues, and writing our Congressmen— calling them to remove the United States from the United Nations, and demanding that they refrain from further entangling our country in unconstitutional treaties that destroy the sovereignty of our nation. We can no longer waste our time and energy on neo-conservative agendas that, in the end, only continue to enlarge the size of government and pave the road to the New World Order.

Finally, we must recognize and oppose the real enemy— big government. When big brother comes, he will disguise himself as an angel of light (2 Corinthians 11:14). However, when we peek behind the curtain we will see him for who he is—Satan, the adversary of God and the enemy of all that is good and true. Big government is not the answer; big government is man's greatest threat, for big government has murdered hundreds of millions of human beings in the twentieth century alone. With the technology of the twenty-first century, big government, if it is allowed to grow, will slaughter billions of innocent people. Therefore, with the real enemy in our sites, we must urge our congressmen to break all ties with the United Nations. Once America is free from international entanglements, we must convince our leaders to shrink the size of the federal government and return to the states the sovereignty stolen from them.

If enough Christians take these seven steps, we can win our nation back. We can once again be one nation under

God. We can return to a biblically based limited government and abandon the godforsaken road to tyranny.

RECOMMENDED READING:

The Declaration of Independence*

The United States Constitution*

The Bill of Rights*

The Federalist Papers*

The Anti-Federalist Papers*

*These founding documents, and others, can be found on the internet at the website of the *Constitution Society* (www.constitution.org).

Brooke, Tal. *One World*. Berkeley: End Run Publishing, 2000.

Eidsmoe, John. *Christianity and the Constitution*. Grand Rapids: Baker Book House, 1987.

Grigg, William Norman. *Freedom on the Altar*. Appleton: American Opinion Publishing, 1995.

Jasper, William F. *Global Tyranny . . . Step By Step*. Appleton: Western Islands, 1992.

Jasper, William F. *The United Nations Exposed*. Appleton: The John Birch Society, 2001.

McDonald, Lawrence. *We Hold These Truths*. Marietta,

GA.: The Larry McDonald Memorial Foundation, 1993.

McManus, John F. *Changing Commands*. Appleton: The John Birch Society, 1995.

The New American. Appleton, WI. (a biweekly news magazine that deals with the New World Order and the globalist conspiracy from a constitutionalist perspective, their website address is www.thenew american.com)

Perloff, James. *The Shadows of Power*. Appleton: Western Islands, 1988.

Spiritual Counterfeits Journal. Berkeley, CA. (a monthly Christian counter-cult magazine that monitors the rise of the neo-pagan one-world religion)

Skousen, W. Cleon. *The Naked Capitalist*. Salt Lake City, 1970.

Many of these books are available from the American Opinion Book Services website located at www.aobs-store.com.

RECOMMENDED ORGANIZATIONS:

☆ *The Institute of Biblical Defense* (a Christian apologetics ministry that specializes in defending the Christian Faith)
P. O. Box 3264
Bremerton, WA 98310
(360) 698-7382
www.biblicaldefense.org

☆ *The John Birch Society* (an educational organization that exposes and refutes the global conspiracy known as the New World Order)
P. O. Box 8040
Appleton, WI 54912
(920) 749-3780
www.jbs.org

☆ *Spiritual Counterfeits Project* (a Christian apologetics ministry that specializes in exposing and refuting the coming one-world, neo-pagan religion)
Box 4308
Berkeley, CA 94704
(510) 540-0300
www.spc-inc.org

ABOUT THE AUTHORS

PHIL FERNANDES

Dr. Phil Fernandes is the president of the Institute of Biblical Defense, which he founded in 1990 to teach Christians how to defend the Christian Faith. He is also the pastor of Trinity Bible Fellowship in Bremerton, Washington, and teaches philosophy, world religions, theology, and apologetics for King's West High School and Cascade Bible College.

Fernandes has earned the following degrees: a Ph.D. in philosophy of religion from Greenwich University, a Master of Arts in Religion from Liberty University, and a Bachelor of Theology from Columbia Evangelical Seminary. Fernandes has debated some of America's leading atheists (i.e., Dr. Michael Martin of Boston University, Jeff Lowder, and Dan Barker). He has lectured and debated in defense of the Christian world view at some of America's leading universities: Princeton, University of Washington, and University of North Carolina (Chapel Hill). Fernandes is a member of three professional societies: the Evangelical Theological Society, the Evangelical Philosophical Society, and the Society of Christian Philosophers.

Fernandes is the author of several books: *The God Who Sits Enthroned: Evidence for God's Existence*, *No Other Gods: A Defense of Biblical Christianity*, and *Theism vs. Atheism: The Internet Debate* (co-authored with Dr. Michael Martin).

Dr. Fernandes honorably served his country from 1980 to 1983 in the United States Marine Corps. His primary duty was guarding nuclear weapons at Naval Submarine Base Bangor.

Books, videos, and hundreds of audio cassette lectures by Dr. Fernandes can be purchased from the Institute of Biblical Defense through the phone number, address, or website and email listed below:

The Institute of Biblical Defense
P. O. Box 3264
Bremerton, WA. 98310-0442
(360) 698-7382
ibd@sinclair.net
www.biblicaldefense.org

ERIC S. PURCELL

Eric Purcell is the Vice President of the Institute of Biblical Defense (IBD) and is an Elder and Praise & Worship team member at Trinity Bible Fellowship (TBF).

Eric has earned the following degrees: A Master of Theological Studies (M.T.S.) from Columbia Evangelical Seminary, and a Bachelor of Theology with a major in Apologetics (Th.B.) from Faraston Theological Seminary. He has begun work on his Doctor of Ministry (D.Min.) from Columbia Evangelical Seminary and hopes to complete that program by the end of 2003.

Eric has taught Christian homeschoolers and church/para-church leaders in many areas of Christian apologetics including: New Testament reliability, God and government, refutation of the theology of the cults (Latter Day Saints, Jehovah's Witnesses, etc.), and Old Testament themes. Eric specializes in the area of Historical Apologetics.

Eric served honorably in the United States Navy from 1987 to 1995 and was decorated for service in Operation Desert Storm. He primary duty was as a Nuclear Power Reactor Operator and Nuclear Power Propulsion Supervisor. Eric still works with the United States Navy as a Department of Defense contractor in a defense-industry engineering design, installation, and repair corporation.

Eric currently resides in Bremerton, WA, with his lovely wife Tina (a constant source of support and strength) and their beautiful daughter Sarah Rose.

KURT RINEAR

Kurt Rinear is a Research Associate with the Institute of Biblical Defense. In addition to research, Kurt also manages IBD's website and video production.

Kurt has earned a Bachelor of Theology from Columbia Evangelical Seminary and is planning to start a Master of Arts in Apologetics program with Southern Evangelical Seminary.

Kurt served honorably in the United States Navy from 1987 to 1998. He works full-time as an Information Technology Manager. He lives in Port Orchard, WA, and has twin daughters Trinity and Victoria.

RORRI WIESINGER

Rorri Wiesinger is a Research Associate with the Institute of Biblical Defense and manages the audio production department.

Rorri has earned a General Bible Diploma from

Faraston Theological Seminary and is completing his Associate of Theological Studies from Columbia Evangelical Seminary.

Rorri served honorably in the United States Marine Corps from 1982 to 1986. He works full-time as a Washington State Corrections Officer and is was a Coordinator for the John Birch Society. He resides in Port Orchard, WA.

Printed in the United States
72627LV00002B/340-387